Come Into the Light

Project
LITURGIAM AESTIMARE
Appreciating Liturgy

Project moderator
Ephrem Carr, OSB

Project directors
James G. Leachman OSB *and* **Daniel P. McCarthy OSB**

DREI Publications
DOCUMENTA RERUM ECCLESIASTICARUM INSTAURATA

Series
LITURGIAM ARTIBUS PROVEHENS ARCHITECTURA
Architecture with Arts Promoting Liturgy

Endorsed by
The President's Council
The Pontifical Liturgy Institute
Sant'Anselmo, Rome

Come Into the Light

Church interiors for the celebration of liturgy

DANIEL P. MCCARTHY OSB
JAMES G. LEACHMAN OSB

CANTERBURY
PRESS
Norwich

in association with

THE
TABLET

First published in volume form in 2016 by the Canterbury Press
Norwich

Canterbury Press is an imprint of Hymns Ancient & Modern Ltd
(a registered charity)
13A Hellesdon Park Road, Norwich
Norfolk NR6 5DR, UK

In association with The Tablet Publishing company,
1 King Street Cloisters
Clifton Walk, London W6 0GY

www.canterburypress.co.uk

Quotations from Vatican II are taken from *Decrees of the Ecumenical Councils*, 2 vols, ed. N. Tanner, Sheed & Ward: Georgetown, 1990.

British Library Cataloguing in Publication data

A catalogue record for this book is available
from the British Library

ISBN 978 1 84825 757 3

Typeset by Regent Typesetting
Printed and bound in Great Britain by
Ashford Colour Press

QUANTO MAIORE SINT FRUCTU
LITURGIAM PARTICIPATURI
UT AESTIMENT FIDELES
ITINERA SINGULATIM IAM EDITA
NUNC COLLECTA
LECTURIS DEDICANT SCRIPTORES

The writers dedicate
to people about to read
the journeys already published singly,
now collected
so that they may appreciate
with how much greater benefit
the faithful are going to participate in liturgy

CONTENTS

III Five ways to arrange a church

Standing around the altar

Table of the Word – table of the Eucharist

Two-part structure of the Eucharist

Basilica tradition

IV The Ritual Model

Font – ambo – altar

LIST OF ILLUSTRATIONS

ACKNOWLEDGEMENTS

This contribution owes its inspiration to Prof. Crispino Valenziano, and introduces an English-speaking readership to his comprehensive vision of architecture for liturgy, a vision which resonates the breadth of the Christian tradition and provides insights into the liturgical renewal of Vatican II. In his research on the ambo, Prof. Valenziano uncovered what lay hidden by accident of history, and from this beginning he has tightly synthesized a prolonged narration on the relationship between the Christian assembly celebrating liturgy and its icon: the church building.

The collaboration of Diana Klein, editor of the 'Parish Practice' page of *The Tablet*, working with Catherine Pepinster, editor of *The Tablet*, and also with the assistant editor James Roberts, was essential in the original publication of these now revised articles. Their insights and ability to address their readership enrich each of these articles. They are responsible for the headings and the sub-headings of each article along with the *To Do* action items. These contributions would not have come to fruition in this book without the backing of Ignatius Kusiak, publisher of *The Tablet*, whose personal encouragement of the authors is heartfelt and much appreciated.

The authors wish to thank their monastic communities, Abbot James Albers osb, and the community of St Benedict's Abbey, Atchison, Kansas; and Abbot Martin Shipperlee osb, and the community of Ealing Abbey, London, for their fraternal support. Thanks are due also to Abbot Kris Op de Beek OSB, and the community of Keizersberg Abbey, Leuven, who have long cultivated the inspiration for active participation in the liturgy and continue to support our writing by their warm welcome and the personal quality of their monastic life.

The remote origins of this book lie in many a Sunday lunch at the family table of Nick and Millie Theis in Troy, Kansas. Millie became a second mother to Daniel McCarthy in the parish where he served as parish priest (pastor) from 1995 to 1999, after the passing of his mother Annette in 1988. Their daughter Margaret Stanton is experienced in parish ministry and assisted Daniel with her gift of helping to ease young priests into their ministerial role. After lunch they would remain at the dining-room table and sketch different arrangements for the church of St Charles Parish until they came upon one of such lasting value as has been proven true by subsequent studies and travel presented in this volume. That insight was the inspiration for rearranging the chapel at Mother of the Church Convent in the following story.

A warm welcome was extended by Sr Mary Thomas and the sisters of *Mater Ecclesiae* Congregation, near Rugby, Warwickshire, where we were allowed temporarily to rearrange the chapel to take some photographs that would illustrate certain principles. A few sisters helped, and they liked it so much that they requested a presentation that evening, and the community soon rearranged the seating in their chapel. We have continued our friendship and ongoing dialogue with this community of women who come later to their religious vocations.

A personal relationship is essential to offering input into the design process of a new church, and so we are grateful for such an invitation extended by Abbess Andrea Savage OSB, and the community of Stanbrook Abbey, who this weekend dedicated their new abbey church near Wass in North Yorkshire. They have erected the first ambo to be built in England since that of

Westminster Cathedral a century ago. They have inlaid Minton tiles taken from their previous abbey to serve as an *axis mundi*, where the sisters will make their profession, share Communion and lie in vigil during funeral services; these rituals occur at the intersection of the liturgical and monastic axes of their chapel.

An invitation to a more prolonged conversation was extended by Sr Anne Shepard OSB, and the sisters of Mount St Scholastica Monastery, Atchison, Kansas, who welcomed Fr Daniel to give their annual community retreat in 2014. He used images of liturgical action, artistic narratives and architecture along with the prayers of the liturgy to consider the mysteries we celebrate. Their ongoing contribution also to the project *Generative Communities* is ever enriching, ever appreciated.

These three communities of religious women, by their conversation, decisiveness and action, have tested and brought to fruition the principles presented in this book; for their invitations to collaborate, the authors remain grateful.

James Leachman's association with Lincoln Cathedral began in his early years when his father would accompany him to Holy Communion each Sunday. James came to know the place in a new way when we were given access to its architecture and liturgy by the Revd Gavin Kirk, former Precentor of Lincoln Cathedral and now Archdeacon of Lincoln, for whose friendship and support we are most grateful. We are equally grateful to the Revd Canon Christopher Tuckwell, Administrator of Westminster Cathedral, and appreciate his friendly welcome in discussion and access to the Cathedral of the Most Precious Blood for photography of, in particular, the magnificent ambo situated in the nave.

While writing these commentaries over the course of several years, Fr Daniel was a guest of Catholic Memorial High School, Waukesha, Wisconsin, and of its President, Fr Paul Hartmann, as well as a guest of St Aloysius Parish, West Allis, Wisconsin, and of their pastor Fr Jeffrey Prasser. Their generous hospitality continues to be much appreciated.

ACKNOWLEDGEMENTS

Our work would not be as accessible or as well regarded academically without the careful and thorough contribution of Br Sixtus Roslevich OSB, a monk of St Louis Abbey, Missouri, who compiled the indices in this and previous books, and in so doing he has helped the reader to gain greater access to an improved volume.

We are grateful to the Drs Michael and Eleanor McCarthy, Oceanside, California, for their support and technical assistance in managing numerous web-pages so that we may communicate these ideas more widely, and especially for their familial hospitality.

The Latin dedication was refined with the help of our teacher and now colleague Fr Reginald Foster OCD, who served as papal Latinist for 40 years. His instruction and then collaboration over the years can be repaid only by the pledge of ongoing friendship and these words of sincere gratitude.

Dedication of the Abbey Church
Stanbrook Abbey, Wass, York
6 September 2015

ABOUT THE AUTHORS

Fr Daniel McCarthy OSB, SLD, is a monk of St Benedict's Abbey, Atchison, Kansas. He studied under Prof. Valenziano and wrote his doctoral thesis on liturgical architecture at the Pontifical Liturgy Institute, Rome, where he now teaches on the faculty, offering courses on the Latin expression and theological meaning of short prayers of the liturgy. He also serves as an adviser to the *Vox clara* committee of the Vatican Congregation for Divine Worship and the Discipline of the Sacraments. He is a guest professor of Liturgy at the Catholic University of Leuven, Belgium. He has served as liturgical consultant to the sisters of Stanbrook Abbey, Wass in Yorkshire for the building of their new chapel, and to the sisters of the *Mater Ecclesiae* Congregation, Street Ashton in Warwickshire for the rearrangement of their chapel. He used this material as the basis of a preached retreat given at Mount St Scholastica Monastery, Atchison in 2014. He is the author of five series of commentaries on the prayers of the Sunday liturgy published in *The Tablet* from 2006 to 2011; the first series was published in book form as *Listen to the Word*. He founded the Latin Summer School at Ealing Abbey, London, in 2005 and co-founded the project *Appreciating the Liturgy*. He is a founding member of the *Institutum Liturgicum London* and serves on the editorial board of *Questions Liturgiques/ Studies in Liturgy*. He has also published in *Ecclesia Orans*.

Fr James Leachman OSB, SLD, is a monk of Ealing Abbey, London, and recently emeritus associate tenured professor of liturgical spirituality and of liturgy and ecumenism at the Pontifical Liturgy Institute, Rome, and guest professor at the Catholic University Leuven, Belgium. He is assistant editor of *Ecclesia Orans*, and on the editorial board of *Questions Liturgiques/Studies in Liturgy*. He is co-founder of the project *Appreciating the Liturgy* and a founding member of the *Institutum Liturgicum London*. He has written articles on the liturgy of the Church of England in *Ecclesia Orans*, on the sources and theology of the RCIA in *Studia Liturgica*, and most recently in *New Blackfriars*, in *Sewanee Theological Review* and in *Questions Liturgiques*. He has written about the way the celebration of liturgy contributes to the human maturation of individual participants and communities as part of the *Generative Communities* conversation on the vitality of communal life.

Other books by these authors

Leachman, J. G. and D. P. McCarthy, eds, *Appreciating the Collect: An Irenic Methodology*, (DREI, LA : AL 1), St Michael's Abbey Press, 2008.

McCarthy, D. P. and J. G. Leachman, *Listen to the Word: Commentaries on Selected Opening Prayers of Sundays and Feasts with Sample Homilies*, (DREI, Varia), The Tablet Trust, 2009.

McCarthy, D. P. and J. G. Leachman, eds, *Transition in the Easter Vigil: Becoming Christians. Paschali in vigilia Christiani nominis fieri*, (DREI, LA : AL 2), St. Michael's Abbey Press, 2011.

Foster, R. T. and D. P. McCarthy, *Ossa Latinitatis Sola ad mentem Reginaldi rationemque: The mere bones of Latin according to the thought and system of Reginald* (Corpus Latinitatis 1), Catholic University of America UP, 2016.

For more information go to:

www.architectureforliturgy.com
www.liturgyinstitute.org
www.thelatinlanguage.org
www.liturgyhome.org
www.benedictine-institute.org
www.college4life.org
www.ealingmonks.org.uk
www.stbedelibrary.org
www.jamesleachman.com
www.kansasmonks.org
www.danielmccarthyosb.com

PREFACE

How appropriate it is that this scholarly yet practical work on bringing the liturgy to life should emerge from the monastic experience. It was in certain Benedictine abbeys in Belgium at the beginning of the twentieth century that the Liturgical Movement was nurtured, and ever since then it has tended to be monastic communities that have led the way, not least because they show us liturgy as the fruit of the communal life of prayer.

It was the monks of the Abbey of En Calcat who first opened my eyes, as a young priest in the 1960s, to liturgy as it could be: a joyous offering by the whole people of God, with music and movement and vesture to match. There all around me was evidence of the sheer intoxication of the whole Church, in the immediate wake of Vatican II, in love with the Word and the Eucharist, exulting in the rediscovered sense of being a holy priestly community called to celebrate and to proclaim.

Monastic communities hold in focus the kind of common life to which all of us can aspire, at least to some degree, in our parish communities; all of us can have this dream, and work to make it real. These essays urge us to fall in love once again with all that we have been given, all that is rightly ours.

When we think about liturgical space, and the architecture which frames our worship and the furnishings which mark and facilitate the actions of the Eucharistic rite, the sycamore in the story of Zacchaeus[1] – a favourite of mine since childhood – springs to mind.

Zacchaeus was a little man in every way, short of stature and shrivelled of soul. Yet as soon as he heard that Jesus was coming his way, he clambered up that sycamore as if he were a child again, eager to catch a glimpse of the man the whole world was talking about. The trunk, limbs and branches of that tree were his climbing frame, enabling him to raise himself up beyond his tiny broken and impoverished world to behold the face of the Anointed One.

And of course it didn't end there. Not only did he see Jesus, but Jesus saw him. And not only did Jesus see Zacchaeus, but he recognized him, called him by name, and told him to hurry on down so that he could come and stay with him that day. More wondrous still than an invitation to eat with the celebrity was this encounter in which the celebrity invited himself in.

Daniel McCarthy and James Leachman have here stripped down and cleaned up the liturgical climbing frame for us, so that we can see more clearly what we have, what we may take hold of, and to what we may aspire. We can walk through the space, touch with our own hands the font, ambo and altar table, and clamber up the structure of our liturgical life to receive the fullness of what these signs contain and point to. Lifted up by our participation in the liturgy, we can glimpse the glory, and respond gladly and eagerly to the invitation of the Lord – no, even more wondrous than that, to the Lord's request that we hurry down to meet him and welcome him into our midst.

This work is timely, for, to misquote T. S. Eliot, the Church cannot bear very much renewal,[2] and whenever habit stifles exploration we all too easily fall back into old routines and defended positions. By a strange coincidence, the sycamore,

---

1 Luke 19.1–10.

2 T. S. Eliot, 'Humankind cannot bear very much reality', *Four Quartets: Burnt Norton*.

despite its grandeur and beauty, is by many regarded as a weed, devalued in proportion to the energy of its fecundity. Likewise the liturgy of the Church is disregarded by many, perceived as an activity to be fitted in when there is time, something to drift through on automatic pilot, rather than the wellspring of all we are as Christians. In the face of this danger of neglect through over-familiarity, McCarthy and Leachman strive to save us from the fate of Esau who despised his birthright.[3]

The authors lay emphasis on five insights of particular importance: on the bodily *nature* of liturgy, earthed in our humanity, in which touch, sight and smell, along with our gathering, gesture and movement are our handholds as we climb up to see Christ; on *reclaiming space*, so that instead of seeing just a church building full of 'stuff', we see a series of distinct spaces within the whole, each with their particular character and purpose, enabling us to understand and appreciate each component of worship with clarity and renewed intent; on *furniture* which through its appropriateness, its simple yet noble design and monumentality speaks clearly of its meaning and purpose for the whole assembly, and feeds our sense of history linking us with those who have trodden this road before us; on *posture*, so that we may look like the community we claim to be, the sons and daughters of God, come of age and taking our rightful place, pressing in around the ambo to hear the words of Christ, standing around the altar with raised hands to offer thanksgiving, using ritual and gesture to express with joy our identity and our calling; on *procession*, so that we never lose sight of the movement inherent in our liturgy, from font, to ambo and to altar, from reaffirmation of our baptismal vows, through immersion in the scriptures, to consummation in the Eucharistic feast, ensuring that worship for us is no longer a static observance but a joyous journey.

---

3 Genesis 25.34.

The gracious tone of the book, using examples from several traditions, reminds us also of the *commonality* of the experience of renewed worship among all who hold the liturgy dear. The wind of change which blew from the Continent in the 1900s was no respecter of ecclesial boundaries or structures, and all liturgical churches found themselves bending in the warm air of the Spirit's breathing. The impetus which culminated in the Second Vatican Council was the same as that which gave birth to the Parish Communion Movement of the 1930s in the Church of England, and to the subsequent wholesale renewal of its liturgical understanding and resources, the same as that which gave birth in the Lutheran tradition to the new liturgical texts in North America, of the 1978 *Lutheran Book of Worship*, and the more inclusive language of subsequent texts. One particular fruit of this journeying together – *The Revised Common Lectionary* – has meant that all liturgical churches have heard and pondered and been challenged by almost identical scriptures Sunday by Sunday, set within a liturgical framework which will appear practically identical to the passer-by if not to the liturgical expert.

By the Spirit of God the renewal of the liturgy has helped place our historic differences in perspective. Distinguishing labels become, if not superfluous, at least secondary before the all-embracing power of the liturgy to engage, inspire and transform God's people.

Transformational liturgy is however not a head thing, a matter of theories and texts and historical knowledge, but a thing of the heart, which can sweep us away with its gentle power. That is why this work is so useful and applicable to all those concerned to see liturgy make a difference in our formation as Christians-in-community in the parish setting. In these essays, scholarly understanding of the theological and historical basis for all we do in the liturgy bubbles over into a host of practical ideas, 'to do' lists, and places to visit and learn from, to help us put theory into practice, in our own small corner, in the here and now.

In this work we are recalled to the heady days of our first discovery of worship, and the authors have such a love for the liturgy and such an eagerness to share, that it is truly an evangelistic book, a further working out of the Good News of Jesus the Christ.

The artist Mark Rothko described his painting as 'an adventure into an unknown world which can only be explored by those willing to take risks'.[4] Because God remains beyond our imagining, and beyond our best attempts to contain or to limit, worship too will always be an adventure. For when we assemble to worship God we begin again the journey which will take us a little deeper into the mystery.

In this journey, Daniel McCarthy and James Leachman here show themselves to be knowledgeable and trustworthy guides, wholly familiar with the terrain, who encourage us to explore what might be possible, in a way which reassures us that it is safe to travel, but which also prompts us to reach for the stars.

Richard Giles
Tynemouth, North East England

---

4 Quoted in Simon Schama, *The Power of Art*, The Bodley Head, 2009, p. 400.

PROLOGUE

This new text *Come Into the Light* by Dom Daniel McCarthy and Dom James Leachman is a source of so much that is beautiful and formative about the way we come together to celebrate God's presence within, between and around us. It is an honour and a joy to recognize the very timely, very skilled descriptions and reflections offered on this collected work.

We are spatial beings, occupying particular dimensions and shapes. Paying great attention and care to the way the physicality of Christian sacred space is provided for means that we are taking the time to respect the outward and visible signs of an inward and spiritual beauty, the beauty of holiness.

Providing for beautiful and meaningful sacred space in this way means that the medium of liturgy will be fully attended to as the context and the means for a message which transforms the world.

This clear, open, enveloping space is a special medium for the healing of the spirit, for the renewal of the mind and for the restoration of life itself. Christ took great care over the physical arrangements of the Last Supper in a particular upper room. So should we.

Come Into the Light offers us, in new and refreshing ways, the profound depths and the great opportunities we have at our disposal from the ancient and modern wellsprings of God's great grace, the springing up of eternal Life itself which is filled with the inestimable riches of Christ, the light of the world.

+ David Moxon KNZM
The Archbishop of Canterbury's representative to the Holy See

FOREWORD

The enormous contribution of the monks of St Benedict to the development of Christian architecture and liturgy is but one example of the gifts that the Church has received from the Benedictine Congregations. Benedictines have built abbeys and churches across the whole worlds and, wherever they have gone, they have brought with them the heart of their charism in the celebration of the liturgy. It is from the roots of this heritage, reflected in today's world by such monastic foundations as Sant'Anselmo in Rome and its Pontifical Liturgy Institute, that this tradition continues to offer itself to the service of the Church in today's world.

This present book of essays compiled by two Benedictine monks, Dom Daniel McCarthy and Dom James Leachman, offers much to all Christian communities as they reflect on their liturgy and on the buildings in which God is made present daily in ritual and symbol, through the presence of his grace. An understanding of the constituent parts of such buildings and the spirit with which they are inter-connected and imbued, enables those who enter these sacred spaces to find the authentic presence of the living God.

Tradition is sometimes misunderstood as solely being a thing of the past, and yet, in its very essence it is a living thing, bringing vital influence to bear on who we are and the journey through life that we are making. For two thousand years God's pilgrim people have pitched their tents along the way, and it is in those very places that God has dwelt among his people. The pioneering work of so many scholars and craftsmen from across the world in the last hundred years or so bears vibrant witness to the ever present challenge of interpreting the divine in the materials of our own day. The challenge continues unabated in our own times, particularly as the gifts and the spirit of the Second Vatican Council continue to nurture and enrich us.

+ Alan S. Hopes
Bishop of East Anglia

Chairman of the Liturgy Committee for the
Bishops' Conference of England and Wales

INTRODUCTION

As a child, my father, George, used to prepare for the Sunday Eucharist first on Saturday evening when his Sunday-best clothes were laid out for him at their home high on the bluffs of the Missouri River. This simple gesture claimed his night's rest and morning routine as part of his preparation. In the morning the family used to walk downhill a couple of blocks to the church and enter through its doors, opening between twin towers. There they always paused for a moment to remember their baptism by crossing themselves with its water and by renewing their profession of faith in the Triune God, 'In the name of the Father, and of the Son and of the Holy Spirit'. Their procession to church would continue as they walked up the nave until they found a pew. There they would pray and listen to the scripture proclaimed and explained. Finally they would resume their procession towards Communion shared at the altar railing. Then they would turn around and begin their journey homeward, pausing along the way first in their pews for a final prayer and a blessing before continuing on their way back home further up the bluff in St Joseph, Missouri.

This simple pattern, ingrained in the weekly actions of people going to church, sharing Communion and returning home again, is brought to its completion by another pattern, that of Christ who comes to meet his people. His drawing near is seen when the book of the Gospels is carried in procession from the altar into the assembly where the Gospel passage is proclaimed as Christ present in the midst of all who hear. Christ draws near once again when the bread and wine of the Lord's Supper are brought from the altar to those who come forward and present themselves for sharing communion in the body and blood of Christ.

This double procession of the people toward Christ, who is ever coming toward his people, leads to an encounter in Christ, the Church's bond of unity. Next, Christ's people turn around and begin their journey homeward so that they themselves might bring Christ's presence into the world.

Well-designed church buildings

Well-designed church buildings support this double procession and provide for the pauses along this journey, first a pause at the baptismal water to renew one's baptismal commitment, second a rest for hearing the Word of God proclaimed and explained before the journey continues with gifts of bread and wine along with gifts for people in their need, all of which culminates as people present themselves to share in Communion. Refreshed by the banquet they return as Christ's presence in their daily lives.

The meaning of the celebration is illustrated by the artistic narrative and architectural design of churches, such that both art and architecture support and interpret the meaning of these simple human actions along the processional way.

Using this book

This book is intended to help the reader reflect upon the inner meaning of these actions and so to participate more fully, more personally in the celebration. Reflecting upon the mystery at work within them, they may perceive its changing meaning at each stage in the course of their lives.

After the celebration has been concluded, the artistic narratives and architectural structure remain as a memorial, a monument to the divine encounter in the celebrating assembly. Visiting a church offers the opportunity to see these monuments and to perceive them as memorials of this divine–human encounter.

Visitors

This book is a guide so that a visitor may read a church building, its furnishings and art, and from these may discern the ritual patterns of human action in the liturgy and their deeper meaning in the divine encounter.

Church members

This book is intended to inspire reflection upon a community's practice of celebrating liturgy and its meaning in their lives. Such reflection may inspire a church community to enhance its pattern of celebration, and to express its meaning in artistic narratives, all supported by the design of a building.

Church building committees

This book will be of service to people responsible for preserving the built heritage of churches by helping them to appreciate the artistic and architectural patrimony at the service of the celebration of liturgy. Understanding how the meaning of a rite is expressed in any given church can help inform priorities when preserving a heritage site. When such a site must be changed, this book may help those responsible to consider more fully the liturgical context and consequences of such change.

National and diocesan commissions

National and diocesan church building and liturgical commissions will have an invaluable resource that illustrates the principles underlying the policies established at diocesan and national levels. The photographs and articles present these principles in ways easily accessible to parish clergy implementing these policies.

Libraries

Libraries will find an interdisciplinary study integrating liturgical science, ritual studies and church teaching along with church architecture, art and decoration. This book provides a distinctive liturgical contribution to this broader discussion already well developed by those versed in the arts.

Arrangement of the book

The custom of my father's family and that of churchgoers all over the world is reflected in the arrangement of this book.

Illumination in the baptistery

As the procession into church first stops at the baptismal waters, so the first five chapters of this book consider the experience of coming to personal enlightenment: coming to awareness and greater insight at different stages of one's life. Thus, the title of this book is *Come Into the Light*. The image on page xxxvi shows the baptismal waters just inside St Michael's Abbey Church, Farnborough, Hampshire, and beyond the baptismal waters is the glorious light illuminating the processional way.

In chapters 1–2, the baptistery is considered as the place of personal illumination. In chapters 3–5, the baptismal font is presented as the memorial of personal enlightenment.

Maturation at the Word of God

The procession continues within this light, and pauses in the pews where people are refreshed by the Word of God, which is the subject of the next five chapters. This contribution draws upon the anthropological research of Prof. Crispino Valenziano of Cefalù, Sicily, into the history, ritual and liturgical development of the ambo, the place from which the scriptures are proclaimed. His research has reclaimed an ancient and common tradition from the first Christian millennium and made it viable once again, especially for the liturgical rites renewed in the past half-century.

In chapters 6–8, the assembly hall is considered as the place of human maturation through reflection on the Word of God. In chapters 9–10, the ambo is presented as the monument of the empty tomb of the resurrection, from which the scripture is proclaimed and in whose light all scripture is interpreted.

Consummation at the wedding banquet

The procession culminates in the experience of consummation, when believers consume the banquet of the Lord and so are drawn into a nuptial union, an intimate sharing in divine life and union with one another. While only chapter 11 is dedicated to this divine encounter around the Lord's table, its primacy ensures that consummation is integrated into many of the chapters.

Six dimensions

The next six chapters consider different dimensions of the celebration. The sun's course throughout the day, its light piercing a church's windows in changing array, suggest a cosmic order to the processions and to the building and its art.

Chapter 12 considers the sun's course from daybreak to sunset as a metaphor for the double procession of Christ who comes to his body, the Church, running out to meet him and of their encounter in the Word proclaimed and Communion shared. This double procession provides a fitting summary to the first 11 chapters of this book.

Chapter 13 considers the sun at its height and its nadir or opposite below, which establish the vertical axis of a church, expressive of the moments in life in which a person transcends a former way of living in order to embark upon a new way of life and a new communion with others as in marriage, ministry, infirmity and in death.

Chapter 14 considers the setting sun as a metaphor for time beyond the day, the dawning of eternity, as an integral aspect of each day's journey. The western facade of a church suitably expresses the eternal values by which we live today, as revealed in a person's daily behaviour towards others, the moral dimension of life.

Chapter 15 integrates the three axes formed by the changing light of the sun throughout a day. The sun's course from its rising to its setting establishes the length of a church from door to altar. This first axis is bisected by the rays of the midday sun cutting across a church and establishing its breadth as the second axis. The height of the midday sun and its nadir or opposite below establish a third, vertical axis of a church. These three axes, the length, breadth, height of a church, give a cosmic order for processions and the ritual actions of celebrating liturgy.

Chapter 16 reclaims the presider's chair as the chair of the teacher and the place for the homily, because the ambo is rightly reserved for the proclamation of the scripture. The ministry of presiding in the assembly and of leading its prayer is also understood in terms of authenticating the ministry of others and receiving their ministry.

Chapter 17 offers a reflection on the sacramental nature of life and liturgy, where the divine presence hides latent to be revealed in ordinary human actions. This dimension is expressed in art and architecture that partly reveals even as it conceals.

Five ways to arrange a church

The final five chapters of this book synthesize all of these elements in five different yet common ways to arrange a church for the celebration of liturgy. The strengths of the first four arrangements are considered as well as their deficiencies, culminating in the more comprehensive fifth arrangement, which we call the ritual model because of its basis in the liturgy as celebrated.

Chapter 18 is based on the ancient Roman Eucharistic Prayer which refers to people as 'standing around' the altar, and suggests that the assembly gather around a central table.

Chapter 19 proposes two tables, one for the banquet of the Lord celebrated around a real table. The other is the metaphorical 'table of the Word' for the proclamation of the Word of God.

Chapter 20 highlights the two-part structure of the Sunday celebration with distinct places for each part, the liturgy of the Word celebrated at the ambo and chairs, followed by the Eucharistic Liturgy celebrated at the altar.

Chapter 21 unmasks the modern tendency to place the altar in the geographic centre of the church, centred under its dome or crossing. In contrast the Roman basilicas of the Lateran and St Paul's Outside the Walls still preserve altars that are off-centre toward the nave, not centred under the crossing or located at the entrance of the apse.

Ritual model

Chapter 22 considers the sequential arrangement of the font, ambo and altar according to the ritual programme of becoming a Christian, first in baptism and Communion and thereafter lived out in word and sacrament. This ritual model incorporates all of the fundamental principles presented in this book that can be applied in a variety of ways for the design of new churches or the renovation of churches for the celebration of the renewed liturgy according to the ancient tradition of Christians.

Afterword and Onward

A brief summary and assessment of the five ways to arrange a church concludes this text.

Photo commentaries

To illustrate the 22 commentaries, this book presents a corresponding number of photos, each with a brief commentary. The photos accompanying each article correspond more or less with the article's subject. Each photo commentary describes one element of a church and gives an interpretation of its theological meaning and an assessment of how it could perhaps be more fully developed.

While each article begins with a theme and gives different examples to illustrate the theme, the photo captions more closely coincide with the experience of entering and interpreting a church. It is hoped that these commentaries will help the reader develop one's own skill at interpreting any particular church.

Come into the light

Come and join the procession. May this book inspire your patient reflection on the architectural design and artistic narrative of a church so that, discerning the ritual patterns of human action in the liturgical celebration, you may perceive their deeper meaning in the divine–human encounter.

*St Michael's Abbey Church,
Farnborough, Hampshire*

Looking through the main entrance of St Michael's Abbey Church, Farnborough, Hampshire. Windows filter the natural light and give it form even as the light moves throughout the day bringing the hall to ever changing life. Light establishes one axis of a church from sunrise to sunset and a second axis as the midday light shines across the church, as seen in this photo. The midday sun seems to stand still at its highest point overhead, suggesting the vertical axis. The movement of the sun through the church in the course of a day suggests the processions and stations of liturgical action.

Outside the church, light often goes unnoticed until a cloud passes by or the trees filter the light thereby producing rays. The church building provides such a filter, and the liturgy celebrated within provides another sort of filter that reveals even as it conceals.

This abbey church is without a baptismal font because it is not a parish. Yet, baptismal water is provided in the marble stand just inside the door so that people may renew their baptismal promises upon entering and leaving church.

I

PRIMARY PLACES –
ELEMENTS – MONUMENTS

Illumination in the baptistery

I

BECOMING LIGHT

Sunlight animates a church, and hand-held candles personalize the illumination as an image of the human process of enlightenment. The symbolism is most potent at the Easter Vigil and particularly so for the newly baptized who receive the light for the first time

Every element of the Easter Vigil highlights the light, radiant in the darkness of this night: the liturgy, the readings, the music, the architecture, all show that Christ's light emerges from the darkness of the empty tomb.

The Easter Vigil begins in evening darkness with the blessing of the new fire, from which the Easter candle is lit and held aloft for the acclamation 'The Light of Christ' and the response 'Thanks be to God' (*RM 2011*). As the assembly processes from the outdoor fire into the church, each person's candle is lit from the Christ candle so that the light increases as it is passed from one person to another. When the Easter candle is placed at an ambo, such as that at Westminster Cathedral, its symbolic structure comes to the fore as an image of the empty tomb where the good news of the resurrection is proclaimed in the scripture readings and in the *Exsultet*, a hymn to Christ the light. During the service of readings, only the candlelight is reverenced as Christ – not the altar, and the tabernacle is barren. This beginning to the Easter Vigil personalizes the light as a metaphor for Christ, as people share the light with others and together they walk in a procession in ever-increasing light.

The Apostle Paul tells us that in baptism we are buried with Christ so that 'we too might walk in newness of life' (Romans 6.4, NRSV). Many baptisteries ancient and modern are recessed into the floor for submersion in imitation of the death of Christ and his burial in the tomb, and then the newly baptized rise from the water to walk in newness of life.

The evangelist John images baptism not as dying and walking, but as being born again in water and the Spirit (John 3.5). Circular baptismal pools are a geometric icon of the Church's womb, and a ciborium or dome over the font, as over the altar, features an icon of the Spirit making the waters fruitful.

The eucharistic hall is directed towards the sunrise, and we go out to meet Christ, the rising Son of Justice, who comes like the sun making its course throughout the day. At the height of the midday sun, from its maximum luminosity, the Gospel is proclaimed from the ambo's empty tomb towards the darkness.

Although proper to all liturgical architecture, the gift of light – that is personal illumination and walking in the light – pre-eminently characterizes the baptistery where we become light. Enhancing the presence of light in the baptistery, a parish may complement the image of their baptismal font as both tomb and womb and place of illumination. At the Lateran Baptistery, Rome, there is an upper gallery of windows directly above the baptismal pool from which rise eight porphyry pillars to support the lantern above. The light above corresponds to the enlightening waters below; such a baptistery is also called a place of illumination by light: *photisterion*.

Adults and children old enough to understand are prepared for the sacraments of Christian initiation by an extended period of purification and enlightenment beginning with the rite of election on the first Sunday of Lent. The three scrutinies on the third, fourth and fifth Sundays of Lent help the elect to examine their conduct and to consider the character of their lives in the light of the Gospel. They receive the Creed and the Lord's Prayer and so are drawn into the mutual self-giving love of the Triune God, in whom they profess faith while standing in the waters of the font.

In baptism, people are buried in these waters and so overcome the tomb to be born again from the waters of this fertile womb. Bathing in this water brings personal illumination because they profess and so are caught up into the love of God and neighbour that they have already begun to experience in their personal conduct and daily way of life.

The newly baptized are given a candle, lit from the Easter candle at the empty tomb, and they are told that they have been made a light in Christ. Not only are they brought into the light, in baptism they become light: 'For once you were darkness, but now in the Lord you are light' (Ephesians 5.8, NRSV). Becoming light is to become like God, for 'God is light and in him there is no darkness at all' (1 John 1.5, NRSV). God's divine Word goes forth as 'light from light, true God from true God' (Nicene Creed, RM 2011). The divine Word is also light for the world: as Jesus said, 'I am the light of the world' (John 8.12, NRSV).

The baptized do not remain at the font, but, when they are given a candle, they are exhorted to walk: 'Continually walk as children of the light, so that, persevering in the faith, you together with all the saints in the heavenly court may be able to go to meet the Lord coming' (translation by author). Ritually this occurs when they process from the font into the hall, and when they bring to the altar gifts of bread and wine and an offering for people in their need, and so for the first of many times give themselves to this way of life, walking in the light. They process with the whole assembly to meet the Lord coming in the communion they share in his body and blood.

Thereafter, they bear Christ to the world. And so the procession back into the world passes by the font, where they bless themselves with baptismal water before returning to their daily lives now renewed by the communion they share with God, with the community and in a new way with their neighbour.

Thereafter, they return with the fruit of their lives to present these once again.

Ephrem the Syrian explains that when Adam lost his original glory, he put off his vesture, robes of light. When Christ was baptized in the river Jordan, he left the luminous garments in the baptismal waters for us to put on in the sacrament (Hymn 7, 5 in *Hymns of Paradise*):

> Both men and women
> are clothed in raiment of light;
> the garments provided to cover their nakedness
> are swallowed up in glory.

To Do

- Consider how we are light to others
- Visit the baptistery (or the baptismal font) to renew commitments
- Enhance the baptistery's natural lighting – especially at the Easter Vigil

Parish of Corpus Christi, Lawrence, Kansas

The baptistery of Corpus Christi Parish, Lawrence, Kansas. Located between the gathering room (behind the photographer) and the assembly hall (seen in the distance), the eight-sided baptismal font stands in the centre of eight pillars supporting an octagonal dome with a lantern at its top, directly over the pool so that its natural light may suggest personal illumination in baptism. The bas-reliefs on the side of the font feature images from the celebrations of the Christian initiation of adults on the Sundays of Lent and during the Easter Vigil.

To the right side are rooms for private reconciliation, from which the reconciled emerge to renew their baptismal promises. To the left side is a small chapel with a stone tower containing the oils for anointing.

People pass through this baptistery when entering and leaving the church. Brides and grooms may pass by the font as they process into church to exchange their vows, and certainly as they leave the church to begin living their Christian marriage. At the end of life, caskets are brought to this font where they are sprinkled directly from its waters with the prayer that what was begun in baptism may now be completed.

2

TOWARDS THE
ENDURING CITY

*The Baptism of the Lord, as well as recalling the start of
Christ's public ministry, this feast – and the church font itself
– are reminders of our continuing rebirth as we make our
Christian journey in search of the Kingdom.*

The year 2012 was memorable in the UK for the Diamond
Jubilee celebrations and for the inspiration provided by the
Olympian and Paralympian sportswomen and men, as well as
by the thousands of volunteers who helped make the Olympic
Games happen. These events and the participants inspired the
whole nation during the summer months: there was a sense of
elation and encouragement.

Thereafter, in the eyes of very many people, political leaders
of whatever persuasion have given the impression that they
have no clear, consistent and enduring message. Policies based
on well-considered principles have been in short supply, while
economic news is depressing. The mood has shifted remarkably
quickly from pride and joy to confusion and discouragement.

For Christians, of course, our nation is not the only realm to
which we belong. God has given us 'an eternal and universal
kingdom, a kingdom of truth and life ... of holiness and grace
... of justice, love and peace' (Preface of the Solemnity of Our
Lord Jesus Christ, King of the Universe, *RM 2011*) to which
we belong. The message is clear. Christians trust in God and,

through their baptism, they belong to God's Kingdom. Our encouragement and our joy are founded on this rock.

Each year the celebration of the Baptism of the Lord comes at the end of the Christmas season. Just weeks before, the Church commemorates the birth of Jesus as a baby; in his baptism the Church commemorates the beginning of new life for him in public ministry. It is one of the major epiphanies (revelations) or theophanies (the revelation of God to humankind): the birth of Christ at Christmas, which revealed Christ to Israel; the revelation of Christ to the Gentiles in the visit of the Magi at Epiphany; the Baptism of the Lord, which revealed the Trinity; and the miracle at the wedding at Cana, which revealed Christ's transformation of the world. The Second Vatican Council inspired theologians and liturgists to write about the primacy of the sacrament of baptism. Many of the baptized have absorbed what the council teaches about the importance of baptism and the liturgical place where the sacramental rebirth as God's children takes place.

In recent years, church architects also have recognized this renewed emphasis on baptism and the dignity of the baptismal font and, in many new and reordered churches, have given the baptismal font greater prominence, often by placing it near the altar table in full view of the entire assembly. Such greater visibility is praiseworthy if it enhances participation, yet a rather different solution recommends itself to those with a greater familiarity with the theological and architectural traditions. In the earlier tradition the font was placed, not in the place for maximum visibility, but in its 'ritual position', the place of its maximum ritual effectiveness; that is, at or near the church entrance. In the earlier tradition too, the font was large and deep and could often be used for baptism by immersion in the pool as well as by the simple pouring of water.

In Rome, the earliest church buildings were named 'basilicas', a name derived from *basilike*, meaning a place for imperial or royal gatherings. Church basilicas were designed for and reflected the arrangement of the Church's worship and the self-understanding of the Church as the royal people of God. Basilicas have several distinct areas: the entrance porch or narthex, the baptistery, the main hall, and the dais for the ministers and the altar. In Mediterranean countries, many older cathedrals, such as the Lateran basilica in Rome, and several churches in Venice, the baptistery is a separate building. The newly baptized, dressed in their baptismal garments, would proceed from the baptistery to the church where the doors would be opened to receive them. There, all those baptized in previous years would await them to join the assembly, the royal people of God, and join in prayer, singing and receiving Holy Communion.

Christians had their own identity as the royal people of God, the elect of God, the children of God, marked out from other religions not only by their beliefs but also by their public and private behaviour. Reflecting on the events of 2012 can help us to begin to understand how important it is to recover a traditional understanding of the baptismal pool, the baptismal regeneration and of the witness as adopted children of God, for indeed the newly baptized are welcomed by the assembly to a new life and a new way of life.

This places an emphasis once again on the careful preparation of candidates for baptism, on the continuing formation of the already baptized for a full, active and conscious participation in sacramental celebrations and on each person's responsibility to continue their Christian journey in obedience to God who promises and enables. Pope Benedict in his most recent book, *Jesus of Nazareth: The Infancy Narratives*, speaks of this new birth and new Creation of which we are part when he writes, '... it can be now said of us that our true "genealogy" is faith in Jesus who gives us a new origin, who brings us to birth "from God"' (p. 13).

The baptismal font (or pool) in churches deserves greater honour. The font is the place of full immersion into the light of truth, and of the filial adoption into the eternal life of the Trinity. As Christians progress through life, they give themselves actively to the changes that occur in them and around them. The font is a reminder of the rebirth into each successive period of life; childhood, adulthood, parenthood and even sickness, old age and death are accomplished through our participation in the life of Christ in baptism.

We are reborn when as toddlers we come to awareness that we are members of a family, when we join a school community, when we consciously join the Christian community, but we are also reborn each Sunday, each year to a new stage of our life journey; and we give ourselves actively and wholeheartedly to our new life, just as Jesus our Redeemer and companion did.

To Do

- Make the baptismal font accessible to all
- Illuminate the baptismal font so that it is visible to all
- Use the baptismal font to remind yourself that you have a new birth and a new identity

Parish of the Visitation, Kansas City, Missouri

The baptistery and altar at Visitation Parish, Kansas City, Missouri. The main entrance to the church is outside the photo on the left, from which the central aisle leads to the altar. The baptismal font is located in one corner of the church, under a balcony. An aisle extends from the font to the altar pictured in the distance, establishing a secondary axis. This axis includes, where the photographer is standing, a wall niche in which a wooden bier (base) stands ready to hold a casket for an all-night funeral vigil at the baptismal font.

Above the eight-sided font, the balcony has an octagonal opening supported by eight twisted pillars (two are visible) that surround the octagonal font centred below. This opening extends up to a slightly recessed dome in the ceiling with a hanging chandelier. Thus, the area around the font is distinct as a baptistery while integrally related to the rest of the liturgical assembly. The font is easily accessible, but not on axis with any of the main entrances and so is less likely to be used for blessing oneself upon entering and leaving the church.

Baptismal font, memorial of illumination

3

A TIME TO BE BORN

In more recent times the Pauline imagery of death and resur-
rection has dominated the liturgy associated with baptism. But
the early Church placed a much stronger emphasis on birth
and rebirth – right down to the feminine form of the font.

The first Christian feast is Sunday, the first day of God's creation and the day of the Lord's Resurrection and of the Spirit's
descent. Yet Christians in post-apostolic times – not satisfied
with this weekly feast – were also celebrating an annual feast at
the time of the Passover, reinterpreting it as the Christian Passover. Recent research has shown that in this embryonic Easter
feast baptisms were celebrated during the Saturday night–Sunday
morning vigil.

This all-encompassing Passover festival celebrated the fullness of the Christian mystery – a double passing: not only the
Lord's passing from death to life and return to the Father but
also the passing of the second person of the Trinity into our
human existence at the Incarnation. So, there were two integral
elements to it: one of birth and rebirth and one of death and
resurrection. This ancient Passover vigil was developed over
the next centuries to reach its full Roman development in the
Gelasian Sacramentary of Rome (628–715). These Easter celebrations were preceded by the Lenten period of prayer and
fasting by the assembly for those preparing to be baptized. It is

time now, in my opinion, to recover the birth–rebirth imagery of baptism and thus to correct the imbalance which has crept in over the centuries due to the preponderance of a Pauline death–resurrection imagery.

By the tenth century the practice of adult baptism had largely fallen into disuse, for almost everyone in 'Christendom' was baptized and thus only infants were brought to the font. Thus, in the absence of the ancient model of baptismal preparation, the prayerful solidarity and the fasting of the faithful in Lent with those to be baptized at the Paschal Vigil came to be sublimated into different purposeful activities. For the clergy, this meant monastic discipline and missionary activity; and for the participation of the faithful, more introspective self-discipline, self-examination and self-correction. When, relatively recently in history, Pope Pius XII restored the Easter Vigil with the renewal of the rites of Holy Week in 1955, he was preparing the way for the rich liturgical celebrations that we now enjoy in our parishes.

The Church has, as mandated by the Second Vatican Council, re-established the public celebration of the sacraments of initiation (Baptism, Confirmation and First Eucharist) during the celebration of the Easter Vigil. We find these rites and prayers for the Easter Vigil both in the *Roman Ritual* and in the *Roman Missal*.

The Rite of Christian Initiation of Adults (RCIA) was promulgated in 1972, then translated into local languages and, as a result of its implementation, we have now come to see more clearly the importance of including the celebration of the sacraments of initiation during the Easter Vigil.

Today we have come to see that the Paschal Vigil without baptism eclipses the Church's fecundity and generative power. When the RCIA is well organized, those preparing for baptism at Easter, called 'the elect', find that the Triduum is a powerful three-day period of experiencing their Christian passing from an old to a new way of living. Just as a child must pass through the waters of its mother's womb into the worldwide community of the human race, so at baptism the elect pass through the baptismal waters and are reborn as members of the new people of God.

Unfortunately, the revisers of the prayer for the consecration of the baptismal waters eliminated all references to the fecundity of the Church and to baptism as rebirth. The eighth-century prayer upon which it was based contained strong theological references to the baptismal pool as an expression of the feminine dimension of the Church's life.

Similarly, in the renewal of church architecture since the Second Vatican Council, the ancient Syrian and Sicilian imagery of the feminine form of the font has been overlooked in favour of the North African and Italian image of the font as sepulchre. In the fascinating yet little-known cathedral of Trapani, Sicily, the feminine form of the font has been recovered. Infant candidates may be immersed in the standing font, whereas adult candidates stand or kneel in a pool surrounding the font, and water gushing from the femininely proportioned font is poured over them.

The Easter Vigil, as found in the *Missale Romanum* (2002), like that of 1970 and 1975, has four parts: The beginning of the Vigil (Liturgy of Light or *Lucernarium*), the Liturgy of the Word, the Baptismal Liturgy and the Liturgy of the Eucharist. These four parts of the Easter Vigil correspond to the four stages of the RCIA journey: the period of evangelization is celebrated ritually now by the whole community in the Liturgy of Light. The long catechumenal preparation is celebrated ritually by all in the Liturgy of the Word. The period of enlightenment and purification is celebrated ritually in the baptism and confirmation of the candidates at the font and in the annual renewal of baptismal vows; and the period of mystagogy and the life of the Christian is celebrated at the altar. Here we have space to look only at the baptismal liturgy. Thus during their whole baptismal preparation, and their subsequent Christian lives, the catechumens and elect pass by stages of human response and transformation from being bound in servitude to the ancient enemy to being free to serve the Lord, until first they are ready, literally, to take the plunge at the Paschal Vigil, and finally in the eschaton to enjoy God's presence for ever.

Parishes will need time to develop the art of celebrating the Easter Vigil. There should be only one vigil in each parish and this should be public, not private. Ideally the ministries developed for the Sunday assemblies throughout the year – servers, catechists, sponsors, readers, singers and psalmist – should be incorporated into the Vigil celebration.

To Do

- Ensure that the ministries such as readers, altar servers, musicians and so on are celebrated at the vigil
- Consider building a temporary pool for Easter baptisms
- Suggest a chrismatory in your church, a defined space near the font where candidates for confirmation stand to be anointed with the Chrism oil

Cathedral of St Lawrence, Trapani, Sicily

The baptismal font of the Cathedral of St Lawrence, Trapani, Sicily. Built according to the Sicilian Norman custom, this font is incorporated into the ambo. The four pillars, whose bases are visible in the photo, support a balcony for the proclamation of the Gospel. The font is positioned in the ambo's empty undercroft, the empty tomb, where the font is recessed three steps into the floor.

The design of the font derives from the conversation between Nicodemus and Jesus about being born again, from above (John 3.3–8). This font was designed as the womb of the church and placed in the ambo's empty tomb of the resurrection, from which Christians are born from above in water and the Spirit. Here infants and adults are born from the womb of the church.

The font and ambo ensemble are situated under the last arch of the nave before the transept crossing, on the midday side of church. On the opposite side of the nave, the bishop's chair sits against the last pier before the crossing, so that the deacon proclaiming the Gospel from the ambo and the bishop standing at the chair face one another.

4

WATER FOR 'NEW PLANTS'

All sacraments derive their primary meaning from baptism, long associated with Easter. Eastertide also serves as a time for strengthening the faith and fellowship of the whole parish.

Christians in post-apostolic times were not satisfied with the weekly feast of the Lord's Resurrection every Sunday. So by the end of the first century they were also celebrating an annual feast at the time of the Passover, which falls in the Jewish lunar calendar on the 14th day of the month of Nisan, regardless of the day of the week, which they reinterpreted as the Christian Passover. This all-encompassing annual festival celebrated the fullness of the Christian mystery, a double passing: not only the Lord's passing from death to life and return to the Father but also the passing of the second person of the Trinity into our human existence at the Incarnation. Next, Christians transferred the date of this annual feast first to 25 March in the imperial calendar, and later moved the feast to a Sunday, celebrating on one day the passing from death to life, which we now celebrate as one feast in three days, the Holy Triduum (Maundy Thursday evening to Easter Sunday evening).

The writings of Justin Martyr (d. 165) show an early association of baptism with this annual festival. Over the next three centuries the rituals preparing for and celebrating baptism grew in beauty, length and meaning. Then, following the seventh century, after most of southern and western Europe had been evangelized (and baptized), these beautiful rites associated with the baptism of adults fell into disuse for many centuries.

Relatively recently Pope Pius XII restored the Easter Vigil with the renewal of all the rites of Holy Week in 1955. Then, mandated by the Second Vatican Council, the Rite of Christian Initiation for Adults (RCIA) was established, translated and put into use.

When the RCIA is well organized, the new Christians who emerge from the font at baptism and thus are called 'neophytes' (the Greek word means 'new plants') find that the holy three days of immediate preparation during the Triduum open up into a further period of rapid growth and change. For now they are not only part of the order of the faithful, but adult – though new – members of the community. There are life-changing implications not only for those baptized; but also this fourth period of the RCIA, the period of mystagogy (the Greek word means 'instruction on the mystery'), is coterminous with the Easter season when it takes on a new richness for the whole parish.

Before I came to teach in Rome, I was responsible for the RCIA at Ealing Abbey's parish, where we made every effort to highlight the baptismal character of Easter for the newly baptized. In this way, the deep symbolism of all that has gone before is opened up and celebrated publicly. At one of the Eucharistic Liturgies each Sunday during the Easter season, I would invite the newly baptized to come and stand near enough to the altar to be able to see what happens there. Many were astounded to be at such close quarters, and to see the nave thronged with the faithful from the perspective of the presider and ministers of the altar.

The *Roman Missal* contains striking examples of Roman prayer formulae appointed for use in Easter time. The octave of Easter has special insertions or embolisms in the Eucharistic Prayers for 'those recently born of water and the Holy Spirit' and these should not be omitted by the priest at the Eucharist (translation by author).

During Eastertide, too, the catechetical sessions for the newly baptized would focus on how to celebrate the Sacrament of Reconciliation, teaching on Christian marriage, prayer to the Mother of God and a day pilgrimage to Walsingham, Aylesford or some other Marian shrine. There was catechesis on the history of the Petrine ministry in the Church and the role of the Holy Father as a centre of unity and teacher of truth, on preparation for ministerial participation in the community and in the liturgy, and teaching on the value of life and on justice and peace, all of which topics spring from the Easter celebration. Thus, we used all means by which we might lead the newly baptized more deeply into the Christian mystery.

Another way of prolonging the spirit of close collaboration that the newly baptized will have developed over their years of formation together is to suggest some form of weekly evening prayer, for which they may wish to take responsibility and to which they might invite the rest of the parish. The RCIA too instructs the diocesan bishop to celebrate the Eucharist each year for those recently baptized.

Celebrations of first Holy Communions and Confirmations are often, with good reason, scheduled for Eastertime, thus expressing the truth that all sacraments derive their primary meaning from baptism. The candidates for both sacraments may sensibly be encouraged to wear some white garment for the occasion in order to heighten the connection. Rather than dressing girls in a 'mini' bridal dress, parents might more properly dress young daughters in a white garment as a sign of baptism rather than marriage – in fact, any white clothing will fulfil the required purpose – and young boys may reasonably be requested to wear a white shirt, and perhaps a red tie to symbolize the gift of the Holy Spirit. Candidates for Confirmation may be asked to receive the anointing standing near the font at a proposed chrismatorium in order to emphasize the close link between the two sacraments.

I have found in my research and writing about the RCIA

and its power to change communities and individuals in the parish that my appreciation of it is well founded. Yet, a parish will need time to develop its art of celebrating these important aspects of the life of the community during Eastertime. All of the celebrations during this period should be public and contain some Easter symbolism – water, oil, fire or white garment. Liturgies, as always, should clearly include a variety of ministries – welcomers, servers, catechists, sponsors, readers, singers and psalmist – in order to express the ministerial participation of the faithful in the liturgy.

To Do

- Ensure that the newly baptized have contact details to stay in touch with one another and the RCIA catechist
- Ask if your parish could introduce a regular celebration of Evening Prayer (see Daniel McCarthy, 'Rediscovering Evening Prayer', *The Tablet*, 5 June 2004)
- Involve the newly baptized and newly confirmed as members responsible for the life of the Christian community

Ealing Abbey, London

The baptismal font of Ealing Abbey, London. The font stands near the front entrance of the church on the main processional way so that people may renew their baptismal vows by blessing themselves with its water upon entering and leaving.

The circular pool is a geometric expression of being born from the womb of the church, while the octagonal form expresses the eighth day. Sunday is both the first day of creation and the day beyond the seven days of creation, beyond history, the eighth day on which Christ rose, when we were recreated: the dawn of eternity. Here people are born again unto eternity.

Beyond the font in this photo, in the niche, an icon of the baptism of Jesus (see p. xxxvi) depicts John pouring water over Jesus standing in the river Jordan, as the Spirit rests upon Jesus in the form of a dove. This connection between the font and the icon derives from the conversation between Nicodemus and Jesus about being born again, from above, in water and the Spirit (John 3.3–8) and shows the unity between baptizing in water and anointing with oil to become anointed ones in Christ, a title which means 'the Anointed One'.

5

CHURCH OF THE SENSES

When Pope Francis blessed the oils used in baptism, confirmation, ordination and the anointing of the sick on Maundy
Thursday, he asked priests to be 'shepherds with the smell of
sheep'. The rich symbolism of anointing deserves better understanding.

A mother lovingly remembers the smell of her baby – and the
scent of all she uses to wash the baby, to oil and powder her.
The child is dependent on her mother and bonds with her and
slowly learns that mother will return if she has to leave her. The
infant learns that, though still dependent in many ways, she is
a separate person – yet, she will have mannerisms and ways of
behaving she learned from family, and will continue to follow
their traditions.

Mother Church, like any mother, lovingly remembers the
smell of her new offspring too. The Church washes her children
and anoints them with the oil of chrism. She dresses the child
in a new garment and feeds the child day by day and week by
week. They will develop a resemblance to other Christians, with
traditions and stories inherited from the church family and with
ways of behaving they learn from the Christian family.

Many have attended at the Easter Vigil and may have wit-
nessed candidates baptized and anointed. After baptism, infants
and young children are anointed with chrism at the font; older
children and adults are anointed with chrism in Confirmation.
The oil of chrism is perfumed and, like the ordained, they will

be recognized as Christians by their scent, their taste, their behaviour. This chrism oil is consecrated by the bishop during Holy Week, together with the oil of catechumens and oil of the sick, and it is distributed to the parishes to be used in infant baptism, in Confirmation and in ordination.

After an infant is baptized, he or she is anointed with a prayer that concludes: 'Almighty God, the Father of our Lord Jesus Christ himself anoints you with the oil of salvation in Christ Jesus our Lord that you may remain members of Christ priest, prophet and king unto eternal life' (translation by author). We hear about these three ministries in the Second Vatican Council Dogmatic Constitution on the Church (article 31) and the 1988 apostolic exhortation *Christifideles Laici* (article 14); they are a part of the Church's doctrine and help us reflect upon the rites celebrated at the font and to appreciate more fully our own baptism.

The anointing of the Spirit proclaimed Christ as prophet, priest and king. Christ assumed our humanity and shared his ministry with us – so, when we consider the risen Christ through the lens of this prayer and the experience of our own baptism, we understand our life in Christ as a divine–human exchange. We are bonded with the divine through the Incarnation, and in response to the gift to God of our humanity we receive new life in return, strength to live in a new way, support from others and a new identity. Jesus is the 'one anointed by the Spirit' – *Christos* in Greek.

The odour of a Christian is their character as members of Christ – prophet, priest, king – and is proper to all the baptized; they should have a smell, an odour, a perfume that gives them away. The baptized exercise their share in the one priesthood of Christ by their full, conscious and active participation in the liturgy and by giving themselves with Christ to God and neighbour. They exercise their prophetic office when Christians act with courage to bring about God's kingdom of justice, love and peace. They exercise their royal office in humble service, as the shepherd who lays down his life for the sheep. The sacrifices we offer include our prayers and apostolic works, our married and family lives, our 'daily work, mental and physical recreation, and even life's troubles if they are patiently borne' (Constitution on the Church, 34, *DEC*). All these provide the odour of the Christian as we live and work with others.

The earliest church buildings in Rome were named 'basilicas', and would have several distinct areas: the entrance porch or narthex, the baptistery, the main hall and the dais for the altar. The baptistery is the place of 'becoming Christian', where the elect are washed and anointed – becoming the priestly, prophetic and royal people of God. They are illuminated and come to see themselves in a new light. The altar is where the baptized come to be fed and are renewed in their baptismal character.

There are two strategies for enhancing the ritual visibility of the holy oils: architecturally and ritually. In considering the architecture of the church building, a parish could first decide, instead of keeping them hidden away in the sacristy, as happens so often, to keep these precious oils in a prominent and secure place near the font. In some parishes I have visited, such as Troy, Kansas, and Potters Bar (Westminster), the oils are reserved in a secure cabinet near the font at the entrance of the church. The cabinet can be locked, and yet be illuminated and visible to those who enter the church building.

A parish may mark a place on the floor of the church near the font with a six-petalled symbol, reminding worshippers of the *Chi-Rho*, where parents will stand to hold their newly baptized infants as they are anointed. A parish may mark a circle on the floor of the church under the dome to show worshippers that this is the spot (between heaven and earth) where they receive the Sacraments of Confirmation and Holy Communion.

In considering the ritual of church celebrations, the diocesan bishop could ensure that sufficient balsam-perfume is added to the chrism at the consecration of the oils – and the priest can be generous in the pouring and smearing of the oil of chrism – so that parents will continue to smell the anointing of their newly baptized child for several days after the baptism. This anointing of infants after baptism does not refer primarily to our resurrection after natural death, but to the character of all the baptized who have arisen from the waters of baptism to a new identity in Christ.

The implication is that when we emerge from the baptismal font and are anointed, we already share in our future glory with Christ as sharers in his prophetic, priestly and royal nature and that we are already becoming what will be fully revealed in us. We are ready to appear in public and betray ourselves as Christians in the way we live as Jesus, prophets, priests and in royal service of all people.

To Do

- Give a secure, illuminated and prominent place of honour in the church to the three oils consecrated by the bishop
- Mark a place of honour on the floor near the font where the newly baptized infants will be anointed
- Betray yourself as a Christian in the way you live as Jesus, prophets, priests and in royal service of all people.

'The Baptism of Christ', an icon by Stephen Nemethy installed in Ealing Abbey, London. Three ministering angels (right) witness John the Baptist (left) baptize Jesus in the River Jordan, where Jonah emerges from three days in the belly of the sea creature (bottom right) and old man Jordan turns back on his course (bottom left; Psalm 114.3).

Ealing Abbey, London

Few churches have a place for anointing after baptism as ideal as this. The oil could be stored in the niche's alcove, secure yet visible. The font is on axis with the icon suggesting a processional route connecting baptism with anointing. The arch over the niche suggests the heavens, where an image of the Spirit at the peak of the vault's ceiling over the person to be anointed would parallel the icon, and directly below a six lobed flower on the floor would establish an *axis mundi*, or pole of the earth, marking this place of becoming a christ in Christ, that is an anointed one in the Anointed One. The flower is developed from a monogram of the first two letters of the title 'Christ', in Greek XP. When the two letters are superimposed, they form six lines converging at a centre point. If the curve of the letter P is replicated on both sides of each of these six lines, then the design resembles the six petals of a flower, as a monogram of 'Christ'.

Maturation at the Word proclaimed in the assembly

6

MIX AND MATCH

Royal dignity, priestly office and prophetic voice character-
ize the life and liturgy of the baptized and the place where
the assembly gathers, whose physical light is reflected in the
liturgy.

The pre-eminence of light in the architecture of a church building is reflected in the use of the metaphor of light in the liturgy.
Equally, the pre-eminence of the Word, proclaimed in the midst
of the assembly, is supported by the art and architecture of the
hall or nave where the assembly gathers to celebrate liturgy.

People gathering to celebrate liturgy are described as grains of
wheat scattered across the mountains, now gathered to form one
loaf of bread, according to the Didache, a church order from the
first and early second centuries. This poetic image is developed in
the prayer, the Preface for a church's anniversary of dedication:
'You make the Church scattered throughout the world to be
built up into the structure of the Lord's body' (translation by
author, cf.: *RM 2011*).

As the loaf becomes the body of the Lord, so also the liturgical
assembly is the body of Christ and its members manifest Christ
to the world through lives of service. This metaphor is the basis
of two contemporary hymns – 'As Grains of Wheat' by David
Haas and 'Father, We Thank Thee, Who Hast Planted' by F.
Bland Tucker.

When a person walks into St James Cathedral, in Seattle, Washington, and approaches the font to remember one's baptism with its water, one steps over an inscription chiselled into the floor framing the font: '… you are a chosen race, a royal priesthood, a holy nation, God's own people, in order that you may proclaim the mighty acts of him who called you out of darkness into his marvellous light' (1 Peter 2.9, *NRSV*). The Constitution on the Church by the Second Vatican Council uses these words to describe the nature of the Church (article 9), as the basis for the richly ministerial character of the entire people of God. This baptismal dignity is the basis for the full, conscious and active participation of the baptized in the liturgy according to a richly ordered ministry (*Constitution on the Sacred Liturgy*, 14).

After an infant is baptized, he or she is anointed with a prayer that concludes: '… so that you, joined to his people, may remain members of Christ, priest, prophet and king, unto eternal life' (translation by author; *see*: Constitution on the Church, 31; *Christifideles Laici*, 14, *DEC*). These three ministries – priest, prophet and king – are proper to all the baptized. The baptized exercise their share in the one priesthood of Christ by their full, conscious and active participation in the liturgy and by giving themselves with Christ to God and neighbour. They exercise their prophetic office when Christians act with courage to bring about God's kingdom of justice, love and peace. They exercise their royal office in humble service, as the shepherd who lays down his life for the sheep.

Jesus said: 'I am the vine, you are the branches' (John 15.5, *NRSV*). This is graphically depicted in the Norman bas-reliefs of the fourth-century basilica of *Santa Sabina*, Rome. One bas-relief depicts a central vine stalk rising majestically like a tree trunk, and on both sides its branches extend horizontally in rows with tendrils curling up and down in alternation, each tendril curling back to form a nearly closed circle, and from the base of each tendril there arises a cross framed by each circle. These crosses are the Christians who have been signed with the cross of Christ, and together they are the Church in her unity with Christ the Vine. Other reliefs convey the same ecclesial message with a more abstract pattern. For example, one looks like a basket weave, where each crisscross, each Christian, is tightly inter-woven into the whole.

This art may appear to be merely decoration on a theme, until one realizes that the bas-reliefs are arranged in the central hall of *Santa Sabina*, the place where the liturgical assembly gathers. The artwork is the permanent expression and reminder of the assembly's identity, which gathers there as the body of Christ, the Church. These reliefs present a challenge to contemporary church architecture and art. Often liturgical assemblies gather in a hall that is ringed with devotional art that has minimal ref-erence to the Church gathered in this space for the celebration of the liturgy. These reliefs suggest the value of art that gives permanent expression to the identity of the assembly that cele-brates the liturgy there.

These bas-relief panels also serve another role, in that they are arranged in the midst of the basilica to form an enclosure in which a small liturgical assembly can comfortably sit. The entrance to this enclosure is nearest the church's main door, and an aisle leads through the seating to the altar just beyond the enclosure's other end.

Built into the north side of this enclosure is a raised platform from which the Epistle is read by a lector facing toward the apse, towards Christ coming in the Gospel and Eucharist both brought from the altar to the assembly. Built into the opposite side of the enclosure is another raised platform from which the Gospel is proclaimed by the deacon, standing with the midday sun to his back and facing with the sun's rays shining across the church. Under this platform is another bas-relief that serves as an image of the Resurrection. This image of the Resurrection and that of the vine and branches together suggest the enclosed garden of the empty tomb from which the angel commanded the myrrh-bearing women to go and tell the disciples the Good News of the Resurrection. This entire enclosure, then, is called an ambo because it supports the ritual proclamation of the Good News during the Liturgy of the Word.

Another type of ambo was constructed at Westminster Cathedral. There, the floral decorations suggest the garden, and the empty undercroft the empty tomb. In both examples, the ambo is located in the midst of the basilica, that is in the midst of the liturgical assembly, as in ancient Israel. When Israel returned from exile in Babylon, the scroll of the Book of the Law was found hidden within the ruined wall of the Temple, and Ezra gathered the whole camp around a raised platform from which he proclaimed the entire Law of God in the midst of the people (Nehemiah 8). These examples of proper ambos suggest the value and preserve the tradition of proclaiming the Word of the Lord in the midst of the assembly.

As light is the pre-eminent quality of the baptistery and of Christian illumination, so also the Word is the pre-eminent quality of the hall where the assembly gathers to hear the Word proclaimed.

To Do

- Decorate the assembly's place with art expressive of its baptismal dignity
- Proclaim the scriptures from the midst of the assembly
- Use the hymn 'As Grains of Wheat' to recall that just as the grains are gathered to form one loaf of bread, we are gathered to form the body of Christ

Basilica of Santa Sabina on the Aventine Hill, Rome

A Norman bas-relief carving in the Basilica of *Santa Sabina* on the Aventine Hill, Rome. Decorative art is chosen for its beauty. But, when the artwork is well integrated into the fabric of the church in such a way that it supports the liturgical activity and expresses the deeper meaning of the liturgy celebrated there, it becomes liturgical art, as here. The place of the baptized in this church is indicated by this artistic statement about the gathered assembly.

The entire composition is of a vine and the vine-branches. Pictured is a detail of two tendrils, each curling around a cross. The ridges carved into each tendril extend up into its cross to suggest they are nourished with sap coming from the one vine stock. Each cross indicates an individual Christian, signed with the cross of Christ first in baptism and then frequently throughout her or his Christian life. The baptized gather here, are nourished here, live from their communion here.

This bas-relief also forms part of the low wall that comprises the ambo. Its vine motif suggests the garden of the empty tomb, imaged in another part of the enclosure.

7

ASSEMBLED AS ONE

Christ is present in the Eucharist in different ways. Here we look at the way he is present in the assembly as a whole, and what his presence means for the way we regard one another when we come together for worship.

While on holiday recently, I joined in the Eucharist in the small church of St Francis, Bardney, in the Lincolnshire countryside. The church building was packed with about 40 local people, and yet, when I was talking afterwards, I discovered that only about ten members live in the village. All the others at the liturgy had come from as far as 15 miles distant to make up the Body of Christ in that small church and to pray. They felt welcome and had responded.

The worshippers, of different ages, had come from different walks of life, and they responded on that Saturday evening to God's call in different ways. There were a farmer, young families, children, teenagers, professional people, some retired people and holidaymakers; everyone felt at home in their church and they joined in wholeheartedly. I saw again that liturgy is not simply the reading of words and the following of rubrics by priest and server; never an act of the celebrant alone. There is no 'audience' of passive spectators who merely watch the priest and the altar servers, and who say their private prayers and devotions. The liturgy invites each one of us to participate fully and actively in our own way.

My home parish at Ealing Abbey has congregations very different in character from the one in Bardney, not only in their size but also in their cultural diversity. Members of many European nationalities, as well as Indians, Iraqis, Iranians, Chinese, Japanese, Malaysians and Filipinos from Asia, and others from North and South America, Caribbean countries and Nigerians and Zimbabweans all call this parish their spiritual home. The parish community takes great care to make sure that all nationalities are made to feel welcome. Each celebration begins with every member of the faithful deciding for themselves to respond to God's invitation and come to the Eucharist, to bring their weekday activities to the assembly, to present themselves and their lives to God and to receive the gift of God's self in return.

There are practical things we can do to make it easier for people to come and join in our liturgies. Whoever we are, whether we live in village or suburb or city centre, the Sunday assembly is created by believers gathering in faith, and we should take active steps to help people to attend.

Some people tend to be overlooked, and more care should be taken to include them in the assembly. Many parishes already take active steps to welcome young people and the housebound, but greater efforts can be taken to include those with learning difficulties, the wheelchair-bound, the blind and those with hearing and speech impairments. The use of sign language at one liturgy can welcome the deaf, while the blind can proclaim the Word of God with Braille texts. Families who have members with learning difficulties can be made especially welcome. A number of reserved parking places for the disabled and elderly can enable them to come to church. Architects could avoid placing steps at the entrance to the church building, at the lectern and sanctuary, for these dissuade the wheelchair-bound from obtaining access to the building and joining the worship, and prevent them from proclaiming the readings and serving at the altar. Unless we make greater effort, the assembly will lack many of its possible members and the Church in her variety and riches is not made visible.

The *Constitution on the Sacred Liturgy* of the Second Vatican Council affirms Christ's presence in the assembly. It declares Christ is present as well in the Liturgy of the Word, in the person of the minister and most especially in the sacred species (article 7). Thus, our assembling is important, and every effort at inviting and including worshippers is to be taken in order that Christ be present, and present visibly to the world.

The understanding of 'assembly' expressed by the fathers at the Vatican Council finds its origin in the Hebrew and Christian Scriptures. In the first scriptural account, dating to about 440 BC, we find that: 'the priest Ezra brought the law before the assembly, both men and women and all who could hear with understanding' and the Jews assembled each day for eight days for the reading of the law (Nehemiah 8.2–3, 4–18, and following; citation Nehemiah 8.2, *NRSV*). Later, Jesus draws people and says 'make them sit down' (Luke 9.14, *NRSV*); he invites his disciples to the upper room (Mark 14.15 and Luke 22.12). The apostolic community 'devoted themselves to the apostles' teaching and fellowship, to the breaking of bread and the prayers' (Acts 2.42, *NRSV*), and Christians ever since have assembled for Eucharist.

In the first part of the liturgy we come together and form this assembly, we sing the entrance antiphon or hymn, and make the sign of the Cross together. The celebrant greets others in the assembly who respond, and there follow both the penitential rite and 'Glory to God in the highest'. Finally the celebrant invites the assembly to pray: there follows silent prayer, the celebrant proclaims the opening prayer, and the assembly assents with 'Amen' (*RM 2011*). With these actions we relive what faithful people have done since the Old Testament times and with these words we commemorate God's saving deeds in the past.

Singing together helps us to pray as one assembly. Common

gestures such as making the sign of the Cross, bowing to the altar, standing for song and for the proclamation of the Gospel, kneeling or sitting, can all bring the different members to participate actively in the worship of the one assembly. As we work to make sure that all are called and all can respond, we shall see week by week and year by year, people of many ages, abilities and cultures – just as believers before us have done – respond to God's invitation to assemble for worship. We are encouraged when more attend and Christ will be better proclaimed when all members of the Christian assembly, whether child, adolescent, adult, parent, midlifer, senior or aged, join together and participate.

All the baptized, of whatever age and condition, are called to join the assembly week by week, and our parish communities can help people to join our Christian assemblies.

To Do

- Observe how people are as they come to Mass – how they present themselves and their lives to God ready to receive the gift of God's self in return
- Consider whether people experience Christ's presence as we assemble for liturgy
- Ask yourself if people in your parish participate fully and actively each in their own way

Basilica of San Stefano Rotondo *on the Caelian Hill, Rome*

The interior of the Basilica of *San Stefano Rotondo* on the Caelian Hill, Rome. The central drum of this church is surrounded by a circular walkway, surrounded in antiquity by a second walkway. The pillars open and unify the whole space, whose circular plan accentuates the unity of the gathered assembly.

The new altar placed in the dead-centre occupies the sole focal point of the entire building. The liturgy thereby becomes more static with reference to this one point. The perennial problem with a central plan is both to create some form of directionality and to provide several places for liturgical actions.

Recent excavations have revealed that this central drum once included low walls forming a processional way that led to an altar standing near the edge of the central area. This provided directionality and left the geographical centre open to serve as an *axis mundi*, a pole of the earth. An ambo was constructed along the processional way whose prominence complemented the altar.

An architecture of light gives priority to the central drum and the primary liturgical activity there. The ambulatory has more subdued light, while the recess where the photographer is standing is darker still.

8

MAKE A GIFT OF YOUR
MINISTRY

It is all too easy for Christians to forget that they are active participants in the Eucharist and to look to the presiding priest as acting alone rather than leading the assembly's worship. Christ is present in the different forms of ministering in our liturgical assemblies.

When I was a child, each Sunday morning after church my father would take the five children of the family birdwatching in Lincolnshire while my mother was left in peace, just as she preferred, to cook Sunday lunch for us all. When the bulging carload of ornithologists returned, the meal was set on the table and we began the family celebration. Each one of us had a job to do: carrying in the vegetables, passing them around, clearing away and making sure everyone had enough. My parents took joint responsibility for the organization of Sunday, we all participated fully and I never even asked the question 'Who is in charge around here?' or 'Who has the most important role?'

Had my mother or father ever been ill, or had one of the children been absent, it would have been inconceivable that anyone could have taken their place. Everyone had a unique contribution. Without any one of us, the event would have had a different character.

The whole worshipping assembly of the Church is richly ministerial, like a family meal or celebration. When we worship in the parish as a Christian family, the gathered assembly is ministerial in many different ways. First, each member brings their Christian witness of the whole week, and, made a member of the priestly people of God through Baptism, offers their life in the Eucharist, 'along with the offering of the body of the Lord' (Constitution on the Church, 34, *DEC*). Second, the parish celebration in itself ministers to the world, making the Church present and visible in the world and proclaiming the Good News. Third, there are many ministries of service to be carried out within the celebration by different members for the benefit of all. What is more, the General Instruction of the Roman Missal refers to 'ministers', and not only the ordained, as having an office or 'service'. So, when the lector proclaims the Word of God, when the acolyte censes the people, when the Eucharist is distributed by ministers, ministries are exercised in proclaiming, serving and feeding.

Catholics are accustomed to having one named person as presider or priest at liturgy. Having a named and recognizable presider gives a personal focus to the assembly. We are also now becoming accustomed to the liturgical leadership given by trained members of the lay faithful, for example in morning and evening prayer, liturgies of the Word, and the rites during catechumenal preparation in the Rite of Christian Initiation of Adults (RCIA). An ordained, instituted or extraordinary minister has responsibility for leading the assembly through the successive parts of the liturgy and for helping each participant to give themself fully to the act of worship. The minister can use a high-key or low-key style of leading worship; this can depend on the tradition to which they and the assembly belong, on their personal preference, upon the needs of the community and on the particular occasion.

The Constitution on the Liturgy of the Second Vatican Council declares, 'Christ is always present to his church, especially during the liturgy, so that this great task can be fully accomplished. He is present through the sacrifice which is the Mass, at once in the person of the minister – "the same one who then offered himself on a cross is now making his offering through the agency of priests" – and also most fully, under the eucharistic elements' (article 7, *DEC*; quoting the Council of Trent, Teaching on the Mass, 2). So Christ is present in the ministers, or rather in their ministering.

Recent official documents have reminded the faithful to honour Christ's presence in the liturgy; and we should indeed remember that, whenever the liturgy is celebrated, Christ is truly present, offering worship to the Father in the Church's celebration, that is in the assembly of the faithful as they worship. Consequently, although the way the one who presides in the assembly carries out that ministry is important, just as important is the way each member of the community comports themself before the mystery of Christ who is present in different ways. When a lector proclaims the scripture within the assembly, the way they live by the Word they proclaim is part of their message. When a minister of the altar serves, the way they minister to Christ's presence in the world during the week is part of their ministry at the altar. When an acolyte or extraordinary minister gives Holy Communion, their service includes the reverence they show before the mystery they are ministering and before the mystery of the others whom they serve.

The place of presiding by priest or bishop is the presider's chair, recovered for the liturgy at the time of the Second Vatican Council. But the other ministers need their places in the assembly, too. Altar servers have seats near the altar, readers can have reserved seats near the ambo or lectern. The cantors can have a special place near the altar or organ or at the back of the church from where they can lead the assembly in song.

Jesus Christ is the one who presides in the liturgy. Jesus was both present at liturgical celebrations in his day, ministered in them and presided. He worshipped as a layman in the Jerusalem Temple; in the synagogue in Nazareth he ministered by proclaiming the scriptures and he kept the Sabbath meal with his disciples. He was baptized by John, celebrated the Last Supper. His self-gift to others in a continual act of service to the world and of praise to God is the content of the Christian liturgy, always giving himself and bringing life to others.

It is time once again that we favour a style of celebration that promotes fruitful worship, worship that encourages attendance at the Eucharist and enables full, conscious and active participation in the celebration. Worship that encourages the faithful to bring their weekday activities to the assembly, to present themselves and their lives to God and to receive the gift of God's self in return, will enable each one to grow in faith and in charity when they return to their daily activities.

Whether in our presiding or in our exercising another ministry, Christ is present, Christ ministers and Christ gives himself in the ministering of the different members of the assembly.

To Do

- Remember that people respond in different ways
- Reflect on whether you bring your whole life to present at the altar
- Practise appreciating the different gifts which the community brings

Lincoln Cathedral

The eagle lectern and *pulpitum* of Lincoln Cathedral. The ambo, as a monument of the empty tomb, developed in a particular way in England. When the rood screen was introduced, it was used as a platform in the midst of church from which the deacon proclaimed the Gospel standing with the noon-day sun at his back and facing with the sun's rays shining across the church.

In Lincoln Cathedral this loft was eventually filled with the pipe organ, but its name *pulpitum* recalls this former use of the space. This passageway into the quire might be considered expressive of an empty tomb, and the balcony above this passageway projects out and has five of an imagined eight sides, like the ambo of *San Clemente* also pictured in this volume.

The eagle lectern is also a remnant of the ambo tradition in that only of the beloved disciple do the scriptures say that, when he entered the empty tomb, 'he saw and believed' (John 20.8, *NRSV*). The eagle, as an image of the Gospel of John, has primacy of place at the monument of the empty tomb in a way that the other three beasts representing the other three Gospels simply do not.

42

Ambo,
monument of the resurrection

9

DISCOVERIES AT AN
EMPTY TOMB

On the Lenten journey, it is worth considering the tradition associated with the construction in churches of an ambo, symbolic of Christ's burial place, and the ways it can be used in celebrations.

On Easter Sunday, the antiphon for monastic evening prayer recounts what happened when myrrh-bearing women came to the tomb early on the third day to anoint Jesus' body. It says, 'The angel of the Lord came down from heaven, rolled the stone away and sat on it. Alleluia, alleluia.' Another antiphon recalls that the angel told the women: 'Do not be afraid ... he is not here.' The Gospel account concludes with the command to 'go quickly and tell his disciples: "He has been raised from the dead"' (translations by author; cf.: Matthew 28.7, *NRSV*).

The difference between a lectern and an ambo is that a lectern, however prominent, is functional: it holds a book. An ambo has a specific symbolic structure as the garden of the empty tomb so that every proclamation of the scripture from this garden and from the empty tomb is interpreted in light of the resurrection and the command to proclaim this good news. An ambo supports the ritual proclamation of the scriptures, affording a finely developed and prolonged ritual narrative.

Essential to an ambo is some representation of the empty tomb. At Westminster Cathedral and at Newman University Church, Dublin, the empty undercroft represents the empty tomb. Other ambos made of solid stone have a design in their base suggesting an empty tomb passing through the monument. The recently dedicated ambo of Stanbrook Abbey, North Yorkshire, has an image of Mary Magdalene greeting the risen Lord.

Justinian's great church in Constantinople, Hagia Sophia, had a monumental ambo with such a large gallery underneath that the choir stood in this empty tomb to sing the hymn of the Resurrection: Alleluia. This provides a creative response to the debate about whether to put the choir near the altar platform or in the balcony. Alternatively, the choir could sing the Alleluia from within the empty tomb, thereby becoming part of the ritual narrative, eliciting the assembly's participation.

The monument of the empty tomb is more memorial than imitation. The ritual celebrated at the ambo only partially imitates the announcement of the angel, because the ritual is developed in ways that express the fuller meaning of the Resurrection. The whole assembly stands for the proclamation of the Gospel in honour of the Resurrection in which the faithful already share, having come up from the waters of baptism.

The minister stands on a stone platform to proclaim the Good News. This platform may be circular in shape, an expression of eternity, or octagonal to indicate the eighth day on which Christ arose to eternal life. Sunday is not only the first day of Creation and thus of history, but after the seven-day week, early the next morning, Christ rose to eternity. Thus, Sunday is called the eighth day without end. Octagons are used for the monument of the empty tomb and in baptistries and fonts, where we are reborn unto everlasting life.

A fully developed ambo also includes the garden enclosure in which the tomb is located. This may be expressed simply by floral decoration, or architecturally as at *Santa Sabina* where the Norman bas-relief stone panels form an enclosure decorated in floral motifs. The iconography of the garden tends to evoke four gardens from scripture, according to Crispino Valenziano, professor emeritus of the Pontifical Liturgy Institute at Sant'-Anselmo, Rome: the garden of Eden and of Creation; the garden of nuptial union mentioned in the Song of Songs; the garden of the empty tomb; and the new Jerusalem imaged as a garden.

A fully developed ambo includes more than one place for the proclamation of scripture. A second raised platform for the proclamation of the epistle is included in the garden enclosure at *Santa Sabina* and at *Santa Maria in Cosmedin*, Rome. Halfway up the steps of such a second platform at *San Clemente*, Rome, there is a landing with a support for an oversized choral book called the *Graduale* because its music was sung from this 'step', in Latin a *gradus*.

In later medieval churches the epistle is proclaimed in the midst of the assembly while facing the rising sun, anticipating Christ coming in the Incarnation and in glory, the same Christ who comes in the Gospel and Eucharist both brought from the altar into the assembly. Standing on a step, the cantor faces towards the assembly to lead its responsorial psalm. The deacon processes with the Gospel book from the altar, following the rising sun into the midst of the assembly to the monument of the empty tomb, where the choir sings the Alleluia. There the Gospel is proclaimed across the church with the sun's rays crossing the nave from the zenith of the midday sun, from maximum luminosity towards the darkness.

The lectionary of our day has been revised and expanded to give greater emphasis on the Word of God. The first reading usually from the Old Testament has been added and chosen for its fulfillment in the Gospel, suggesting that it be proclaimed as the lector faces the empty tomb from which the Gospel is proclaimed.

The ambo need not exclude women or lay ministry. At the

Pope's stational Eucharist for Ash Wednesday celebrated at *Santa Sabina*, two readers and a psalmist including women, and the deacon proclaim their respective readings from the ambo. The abbess of Stanbrook Abbey proclaims the Sunday Gospel from the ambo during the office of readings early on Sunday morning, the same time when the women came to the empty tomb.

A parish may proclaim the scriptures from an empty tomb, especially during the Easter season. The primary floral display could be arranged around the empty tomb as its garden. The Easter candle properly stands at the empty tomb during the Easter season. The Exultet is sung from there at the Easter Vigil, and from there, too, the choir could sing the Alleluia. The tomb could be located in the midst of the assembly, as at Westminster Cathedral and Stanbrook Abbey. Catechesis can include proclaiming the scriptures from the empty tomb, thereby integrating liturgy with handing on the faith.

To Do

- Proclaim the Easter Gospels from an empty tomb in the midst of the assembly
- Get the choir to sing the Alleluia at the empty tomb
- Let the children see the empty tomb and hear the story

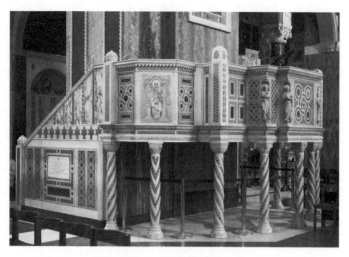

Westminster Cathedral, London

The ambo of Westminster Cathedral, London. The dedicatory inscription (lower left) calls this a *pulpitum*. Yet a pulpit is designed for teaching true doctrine in the sermon. The bishop suitably teaches while seated in the chair, the cathedra. This ambo was designed as a monument for proclaiming the scriptures from the empty tomb, as the Angel commanded the myrrh-bearing women to tell the disciples the Good News.

The deacon processes from the altar carrying the book of the Gospels, ascends the stairway to the left and stands in the central balcony, pictured on the far right, to proclaim the Gospel facing across the nave. The low wall there has an image of the victorious lamb that was slain, which is a positive expression of the resurrection, whose negative expression is the empty undercroft, the empty tomb, sometimes mistakenly used for storage.

The ambo is built against one of the main piers of the nave, two-thirds of the way up from the main entrance. Two distinct places of celebrating the two parts of the liturgy are well developed here: the Liturgy of the Word at the ambo in the nave and at the chairs; the Eucharistic Liturgy at the altar.

RAISE UP THE WORD

The scripture readings mediate Christ's presence in the Mass and need to be proclaimed with power, but this is not always the case. Ministers of the Word must be well prepared, but the point of delivery is important too, symbolically as well as acoustically.

Most of us can remember examples of the power and impact for good of the spoken word. We might remember the first time our mother or father told us that they loved us and how transforming those powerful words were. We might remember the wake or funeral of grandparents or others of our beloved dead and how we shared our fond stories and came to realize how decisive a part the departed played in our own story. We might remember how someone's carefully composed question asked us how we had accomplished a difficult task and how that careful questioning and listening gave us a deeper appreciation of our own human strengths, such as hope, perseverance or self-discipline. In each of these examples, the speaker must be present to us and audible, the message must be convincing and we need to give our attention and respond to it. The human word when spoken in love and truth has power to change us.

On the other hand, few of us can remember examples of liturgical proclamations of the Word of God. On such few occasions as I can remember, the proclamation of the Word was accompanied by a gesture and had a personal power. The content of the scripture somehow made contact with me through the person proclaiming. Just as in human conversation, many aspects of communication need to function well to enable the Liturgy of the Word to communicate its content and to have an impact upon us. When it works well, the Liturgy of the Word can function as a mediation of Christ's presence.

In both human speech and liturgical proclamation, someone we love or respect will capture our attention far better than a stranger; the speaker must be present, visible and clearly audible; the message must be convincing; and we need to give our attention to it. The Lord is always speaking to us; but in order for us to hear and act upon what we have heard, we need the proclaimer, the message and the receiver all to function well.

The *Constitution on the Sacred Liturgy* of the Second Vatican Council declares of Christ: 'he is present through his word in that he himself is speaking when scripture is read in church' (article 7, *DEC*). Thus, our actively participating in the Liturgy of the Word is important, and every effort at helping the worshippers is to be taken in order that Christ be known to be present, and be present visibly to the world through the ministry of the Church.

There are practical steps we can take to make the proclaimed Word of God a living word of Christ for worshippers. Many church buildings have a good sound system that can be a great help if it is well tuned, maintained and well used; though in some well-designed church buildings a sound system may not be necessary. The good preparation of ministers of the Word and of the ordained is also important.

After the opening prayer of the liturgy, the celebrant sits in the chair for the second part of the liturgy to listen to the readings, and the other members of the assembly also sit to listen. We listen to the Word of God, sitting for the first reading, gradual psalm and second reading. The acclamation of the Gospel is proclaimed in song and we stand to greet the Gospel. The homily is properly given by the presider from the chair.

One suggestion, as yet only rarely implemented in the

English-speaking world, is the return to proclaiming the scriptures from a classical ambo instead of a lectern. A lectern is merely a book-stand. The classical ambo, dating from the fourth and fifth centuries, is, on the other hand, a monument of the Resurrection and recalls the stone upon which the angel sat to proclaim the Good News of the Resurrection to the myrrh-bearing women. Thus an ambo properly has an empty space beneath, suggesting the empty tomb from which the Lord has risen. In the fourteenth century, ambos were dismantled, and after the Reformation pulpits were constructed for preaching doctrinal truth. Thus, preaching doctrine supplanted the ritual proclamation of the Good News.

Just as some parishes commission a temporary immersion font each year for the Easter Vigil liturgy, this year they could also ask a local carpenter to construct a temporary ambo in time for the Easter season. Classically, it would be situated under the first arch from the altar on the side of the midday sun (south) of the nave. A simple construction would consist of an octagonal plywood base imaging the stone rolled away from Christ's tomb, its eight sides suggesting the eighth day – the day of the Lord's Resurrection. Three walls of the octagon would be raised on both the nave and aisle sides, thus creating a place for proclamation. The lower side walls of the ambo can be decorated with images of the empty tomb. A ramp could provide access from the altar side to allow wheelchair-bound readers to proclaim the scriptures. The platform would also be large enough to accommodate a deacon and candle-bearers. The different readers of the Word of God would ascend from the altar side, proclaim the reading while standing above the empty tomb and descend on the side towards the church door. This movement indicates that Christ, the rising sun of Justice, comes to encounter the assembly in the Word proclaimed and that the Good News goes out to all the world. Developing such a sustained ritual pattern would support the message.

The renewed ambo could be used at funerals to give the context of the Resurrection to the whole celebration, and at Morning and Evening Prayer for readings and intercessions. The Easter candle stands at the ambo from the Exultet sung during the Easter Vigil until the Ascension, and the Alleluia returns after Lent when it, too, is proclaimed from the empty tomb, at the ambo. All these uses thus emphasize that all scriptures when read in church are proclaimed in the context of Christ's Resurrection. With such ritual celebration, we relive what the faithful have done since the beginning of the Church, and with the words proclaimed we commemorate God's saving deeds in the past, which, when received, are active among us today.

To Do

- Commission a temporary and experimental ambo for the proclamation of the Word for the coming Easter season
- Ensure that rich ceremony accompanies the proclamation of the Word
- Be aware that the lives of those proclaiming the Word are part of the message proclaimed

Basilica of San Clemente, *Rome*

The monument of the empty tomb in the Basilica of *San Clemente*, Rome. The deacon processes from the altar (not pictured at the right), ascends the steps (right) and stands in the balcony, facing across the church toward the photographer, to proclaim the Gospel. The balcony has three visible sides, another three on the far side of the monument and the remaining two sides comprise the entrance and exit, for a total of eight sides, suggesting the eighth day, the day of resurrection. The balcony extends over an oval of dark marble inset into the base as an image of the empty tomb. After the proclamation, the deacon descends the stairs (left), where the Easter candleholder stands.

As in older churches whose apses face toward the sunset, this monument stands on the left side of the basilica, the side of the midday sun so that the deacon may proclaim the Gospel facing with the sun's rays shining across the church.

This ambo in the midst of the nave allows for the celebration of the Liturgy of the Word at the ambo and chairs, next the Eucharistic Liturgy is celebrated at the altar in its distinct part of the church.

Consummation at the wedding banquet

11

TO AND FROM THE LIVING WATERS

Encounters with Christ in the Eucharist enrich encounters with others, in the rhythms of reflection and celebration, proclamation and action, and as God responds with the gift of the Spirit.

Processing to the altar with gifts and returning as gift for the life of the world is the ebb and flow, the summit and source of daily lives of humble service. The faithful come from their daily practice of the Christian life to participate in the Eucharist which in turn nourishes them for their return to daily life. It is like the water lapping on the beach ever revealing something new – and sharing in the Eucharist provides a privileged opportunity to reflect on one's own behaviour and attitudes. Enlightening insights allow for a gradual maturing over the course of one's life, ever coming to know oneself before God and in the Christian community so as to draw from this source the nourishment needed to live anew.

Every liturgical celebration shares in this ebb and flow, as does the celebration of the Eucharist in its particular way, because to consume the body and blood of Christ in the Eucharist is also to consummate one's union with Christ and with his body the Church. Communion shared, then, is the consummation of becoming a Christian through the Sacraments of Baptism and Confirmation, and from this summit the faithful draw as from a living spring an awareness of themselves as graced by God. This sustains their daily practice of humble service in the human family.

This is why the primary processional route in a church is from the front door to the altar and then from the altar back through the front door and into the world. At the beginning of this processional route is normatively the baptistery with its fountain of living waters and the holy oils for the anointings in God's Spirit; there, not only do Christians die and rise with Christ to walk with him in newness of life, they are born again of water and the Spirit, and, so enlightened, they continue to walk in the wonderful light of this truth revealed in them and their encounters with others.

The baptized pass by the font and bless themselves with its waters to recall their dignity as they continue the procession; but before they approach the altar, they pass through the hall where the royal people gather to hear the Word of God proclaimed, to which the holy priesthood of all the baptized respond according to their rich variety of ordered ministries.

The procession reaches its climax as the celebration progresses to the banqueting hall where the Lord's table is prepared for giving thanks. Cyril of Jerusalem described this destination as a thalamus, or nuptial bedchamber, where the newborn in baptism are nourished on the body and blood of Christ, and I like to extend his metaphor to suggest that when the children of God mature into adult Christians, they frequent this chamber as spouse.

Because the consummation of this union is intended to be fruitful, the procession returns by way of the baptistery, through the front door and back into the world for which the faithful have been renewed for their daily way of life and expect that every encounter with another person is an opportunity not only to find Christ in the other but also to draw them into this personal communion.

This rhythm of reflecting on the Word and celebrating the sacrament offers a model to the daily practice of the Christian life by alternating moments of proclamation and action, reflection and ministry, which over time, like the water distilling to crystal clarity, helps people to sift through their life's experiences.

This ebb and flow of the procession to and from the altar expresses ritually another summit and source that occurs in the personal encounter, which is the liturgy. When the procession arrives at the altar, the gifts are brought and placed thereupon. Prayers over the gifts acknowledge that each is the product of human culture that cultivates the vine and grain, whose harvest is fashioned through human labour into bread and wine.

Along with these gifts, the fruit of their labour, the faithful present themselves at the altar. Often an offering for the care of those in need is also given so that the entire Christian life is presented personally at this summit. Indeed, many early churches had altars in the form of a cube, a symbol of Creation because of its limits and surfaces broken at angles. A cube is open to the four ends of the earth, and access is granted to all of Creation and all human activity to be presented along with the faithful themselves at such an altar.

The totality of human life is brought to this centre: daily works and prayers, ministries of service and married and family life, daily occupations, yes also the hungers and sufferings and privations of people, so that all who eat of the common loaf and drink of the one chalice may acknowledge anew their communion with one another throughout all of life's trials and sorrows.

The divine response to this encounter is the ongoing gift of the Spirit. Many people are familiar with the baldachin over the altar at St Peter's Basilica, Rome. Its design reflects the tent of the meeting in which the Spirit of God dwelt in Israel's encampment during the sojourn in the wilderness. Centred on the ceiling of that baldachin is an image of a dove, the Holy Spirit, with rays that radiate out. The statement is clear, the Spirit broods over this altar and incubates the gifts placed beneath. This iconography is developed on a parish scale at St Paul's, Bow Common in London, where the tent over the altar is made of cloth.

The same idea is expressed in a ciborium, for example the domed arch that spans above the altar at Westminster Cathedral. On the ceiling of that arch, at its summit, an image of a dove expresses the action of the Spirit in every liturgy, and especially in the Eucharistic Liturgy transforming the gifts so that all who share in this Communion may be made one body, one Spirit in Christ.

This interpersonal encounter draws a person into communion with others, a communion that is ever respectful of the other person's difference. Such interpersonal communion and respect of personal difference is the consummation of the Christian life, an image of the life of the Divine Trinity, whose three distinct persons share a bond of essential unity. This way of being in relation with others is the summit and source from which the faithful draw nourishment so that they may conduct their lives in humble service to the people they encounter, whom they thereby draw into this life of communion.

To Do

- Help the congregation to process and to experience the symbolism en route
- Include offerings for those in need, along with the bread and wine
- Consider the ways in which action, to be fruitful, needs prayer and reflection, and the ways in which sacramental celebration necessarily leads to action

Cathedral of St Lawrence, Trapani, Sicily

The altar and ciborium of the Cathedral of St Lawrence, Trapani, Sicily. The altar is a cube of marble with bas-reliefs on four sides. The ciborium arches over the altar, with a geometric starburst design under its vault to indicate the gift of the Spirit upon the gifts placed directly below on the altar. The dais is a round platform of a single step, no larger than necessary to accommodate the four pillars of the ciborium. The entire ensemble is installed under the triumphal arch of the apse.

This cross-shaped basilica has a dome over the central crossing. The altar does not occupy the central place under the dome, which would make liturgy more static and diminish other places of liturgical action. Rather, the central open space functions as an *axis mundi*, or pole of the earth. The dome stands above the assembly gathered below, as the ciborium arches over the gifts upon the altar. Both suggest the gift of the Spirit upon the gifts, upon the assembly that shares Communion at this table.

The bishop's chair stands against the nave's last pier facing across the church toward the ambo standing under the last arch of the nave.

II

SIX DIMENSIONS

Double procession toward encounter

INTIMATE ENCOUNTERS

Christ's coming is remembered at Advent and Christmas; his coming in the Incarnation, in the Eucharist and at the end of time can be recalled more vividly through subtle changes to the liturgy.

One outstanding memory of the papal visit to the UK in 2010 was the quality of the Eucharistic Liturgy celebrated in Westminster Cathedral, including the procession of the deacon with the book of the Gospels.

Beginning at the chair where he received the blessing from the Pope, the deacon ascended the steps of the altar, where the book of the Gospels was resting, and holding it high he processed from the altar down the steps into the middle of the nave – the assembly turning as the Gospels passed by – and ascended the ambo. There he proclaimed the Gospel facing not towards the front door but perpendicularly across the basilica: the Gospels had come into the middle of the assembly.

Christ comes to us; this is one of the hallmarks of the Advent season, which begins with the expectation of Christ coming in majesty and ends with the feast of Christ coming in humility, as the babe in the manger. A third, intermediate coming of Christ occurs in the liturgy, as the procession with the book of the Gospels manifests clearly.

Christ is the one coming, whom the faithful run out to meet.

This double procession is described in the Collect on the first Sunday of Advent, whose Latin text says that God's faithful are 'running with good works to meet your Christ, the one coming [*venienti*]' (translation by author). The new vernacular prayer changes the nature of the Latin participle here so that it no longer describes an ongoing process occurring even now, but postpones the action to a single point in time: 'at his coming' (*RM 2011*). By pointing to the coming of Christ at the end of time, the vernacular prayer misses out on Christ coming in this liturgy.

Christ comes to us when his body and blood are brought from the altar to be shared; the faithful come forward in procession to the altar where they meet their Lord, the one coming. This double procession leads to an encounter in which the faithful become more fully who they are as the body of Christ.

Parishes, with only subtle changes to the way they celebrate the liturgy, can enhance how they enact this double procession so that the ritual actions themselves express their reality more clearly. In many parishes, it is common for the altar to be flanked by the presidential chair on one side and the lectern on the other side – the ministers standing at each facing towards the nave, towards the people. The procession with the book of the Gospels, consequently, is a movement to the side of the altar and not a procession into the middle of the assembly. Parish communities reflecting on the experience of the papal Mass might consider situating their lectern in a place corresponding to the ambo of Westminster Cathedral – if not permanently, perhaps for the Easter season, so that they might develop a fuller ritual expression.

Parishes could more easily reconsider how the Communion procession occurs so that it expresses more fully the double procession of Christ and his body, the people of God, and their encounter in shared Communion. The procession of the faithful to the altar might be more fully expressed especially when there are no barriers to approaching the altar. People are often surprised when they go to St Peter's, or the Lateran basilica, or St Paul's Outside the Walls in Rome, and are able to approach very near to the altar because people are not prohibited by an expansive platform or railings. The procession of the body and blood of Christ from the altar to meet the faithful, in my experience, is often done in a functional manner, but perhaps reflection may lead to a greater awareness of this simple rite's significance.

At Stanbrook Abbey church, North Yorkshire, the place where people share Communion is indicated by a design on the floor at the spot where the two processions meet, where the faithful receive the body and blood of Christ. A place of such significance warrants some architectural expression, however simple, so that the action may occur there with greater awareness and intention, and even after the liturgy is completed the design there may continue to proclaim the mystery that occurs.

Christ comes to us in our neighbour, and this coming is reflected in several prayers of the Advent season, lest our liturgical encounter be alienated from our daily lives. The above cited image of the faithful 'running with good works to meet your Christ' is an allusion to the only account of the final judgement in any of the Gospels, when Christ says: 'Just as you did it to one of the least of these who are members of my family, you did it to me' (Matthew 25.31–46; citation verse 40, NRSV). The faithful bring not only gifts of bread and wine but also an offering for people in their need to be used by the Church in her ministry of service to others.

On the same Sunday, the Prayer after Communion in the Latin describes the liturgical assembly as walking among things passing away, asking to love heavenly realities and to cling to things going to endure. The liturgy teaches the assembly how to conduct one's daily life in light of the mysteries celebrated, and such conduct accompanies one in the procession to receive the body and blood of Christ at the altar, and is an integral part of the Communion shared with God, with the faithful and with one's neighbour.

In this way, the procession of the gifts of bread and wine to the altar along with an offering for the neighbour in need take on a fuller reality.

This points to another coming of Christ in the liturgy. Not only are gifts brought to the altar for the Church to use in its ministry to people in their need, but also, when the faithful approach the altar and share in Communion, they are changed into Christ whom they receive; only then do they turn to walk away from the altar to return to their places, and at the end of the liturgy they turn and continue the procession from the altar past the baptismal font out of the door and back into the world. The faithful bear Christ to the world; they manifest Christ to others through their comportment and actions, their selfless service of neighbour, their personal, even bodily, presence to another.

To Do

- Enhance the procession with the book of the Gospels to show how Christ comes to us in the Word
- Reflect on the double procession of Christ and his body, the people of God, and on our encounter in shared Communion
- Consider ways of showing how Christ comes to us in our neighbours

St Peter and St Paul Parish, Salle, Norfolk

The chancel of St Peter and St Paul Parish, Salle, Norfolk. Morning light enters the church through the great window. The morning canticle, the *Benedictus*, acclaims Christ coming as 'daybreak from on high', who 'will visit us to shine on those who sit in darkness and death's shadow, to guide our feet into the path of peace' (Luke 1.78–79; *RNAB*). Evening light enters through the church's facade by a lesser window over the main entrance. The light shining through these two windows establishes the main axis of the church and the primary action of the liturgy: Christ coming as the daybreak from on high and the faithful coming to meet him.

In churches where the altar stands under the sunrise window, Christ comes with the morning sun both as the book of the Gospels is processed from the altar to the ambo, and as the holy gifts are brought from the altar to be shared among the people, who come to this encounter. Then they turn around and go with the sun, bringing Christ to the world.

The place of encounter may be developed artistically and architecturally by creating an axis of the world (*axis mundi*) or a pictorial narrative of the double procession and the divine–human encounter.

Axis of the world

13

CAUGHT BETWEEN
HEAVEN AND EARTH

How a church building is arranged has an impact on how we worship together and can help us more readily enter the mysteries we celebrate.

The earth opened to receive its Saviour and the heavens proclaimed his glory. In a cave in Bethlehem Jesus was born, and the star above guided travellers from afar. The low and high, zenith and nadir, are also paired in the baptism of Jesus; he went down into the waters, and when he came up from the river the heavens opened; the Spirit came down upon him and the voice came from heaven. Again, on Holy Saturday, the Church is mindful of Christ's descent among the dead and his Resurrection and Ascension from the grave, his ascent from the depths to the right hand of God Almighty. The liturgy imitates ritually his passage from below to on high in baptism when, for example, babies being baptized are lowered into the waters and then raised up, or when adults walk down into the baptismal pool and rise from the waters to walk in newness of life.

This passage is expressed architecturally when baptismal fonts for immersion are recessed in the floor of a free-standing baptistery with a dome rising above and its lantern providing light; for example, the free-standing baptistery at the Lateran basilica in Rome has a font set into the floor, and the entrance on one side has three steps down and the exit on the other three steps up. Around that baptismal pool stand eight porphyry columns that support an octagonal drum and lantern above. From this *omphalos* – 'navel' or 'belly button' – all are reborn, the world is renewed.

Christ's passage from the netherworld to on high is given architectural expression in the Church of the Holy Sepulchre which Constantine ordered to be built in Jerusalem. Soon thereafter, a shrine was built around the tomb carved out of the living rock. Soaring above the aedicule is the newly restored dome with its oculus. To enter into the empty tomb is as if to be caught up in Christ's ascent from among the dead to life on high.

In Constantinople, Justinian built the basilica of St Irene which incorporates the cruciform floor plan with a dome over the crossing. From the centre of the crossing to the centre of the dome, the vertical axis remains empty and accessible. At the great church, Hagia Sophia, the dome and half-domed apses came to predominate. There, the altar was placed in an apse, and the area under the centre of the dome was left empty so that people might stand freely in this vertical axis.

In some churches, the design of the floor pavement mirrors that of the dome, as if to indicate that just as the dome rises above, so too the floor descends below, and anyone drawn to stand upon the central disc is, as it were, suspended between heaven above and the depths below, and caught up in Christ's ascent from the netherworld to on high.

This vertical dimension of a church building or baptistery projects a three-dimensional metaphor for coming to share in divine life, as in the Incarnation, when humanity was wed to Christ's divinity, and baptism when new daughters and sons are generated in Christ the beloved Son of God, and the Resurrection, when humanity in Christ rose from among the dead and is now seated at the throne of glory.

In a church, such an axis is marked by a foundation stone upon which the baptized receive Communion, enter into marriage, profess religious vows, are ordained, the sick are anointed and where their mortal remains may rest for the vigil until the morning celebration of the Eucharist, an image of awaiting to join the heavenly banquet, the wedding feast of the lamb. As the world rotates around its North and South Poles, this liturgical pole attracts all our daily activities into its ambit.

Unfortunately, in order to bring the altar closer to the people, many churches were rearranged with what architects sometimes call a 'centre-thrust stage', and many of the significant sacramental encounters such as marriage, ordination and profession are staged in the sanctuary with primary emphasis given to the ability of people to see, as if it were theatre, rather than establishing in the architecture of the building an *axis mundi*, 'axis of the world', and welcoming people there to celebrate rites in such a way that all can participate fully, consciously and actively.

In many churches the centre of the crossing, the place beneath the dome or under the highest or central point of the ceiling, is occupied by the altar surrounded by a raised apron that keeps people away. This conflates the vertical axis of the church hall with the vertical axis that once was formed by the altar and its ciborium or baldachin now stripped away, thereby creating a unidimensional space that keeps people away and gives such emphasis to the altar as to diminish the place for all other liturgical celebrations.

The first step in reclaiming an *axis mundi* is to acknowledge the rituals celebrated in their de facto places of ritual activity and to indicate these even in a simple way. For example, the place where people receive Communion may be marked simply by a disc or a circle drawn on the floor. Reclaiming different spaces for different rites may involve restoring some form of a ciborium over the altar so that it may be displaced from such a central place to the end of a processional way, thereby vacating the 'axis of the world' or *axis mundi* for people and other rites.

A floor design can be sufficient to mark the spot where people give themselves in communion with God and neighbour. For example, the floor design alone, a recently restored mosaic quincunx before the altar of Westminster Abbey, establishes a world axis for the coronation of the English monarch.

To Do

- Identify the crossing points in the floor and ceiling of a church and mark them
- Make the most of this space by celebrating Communion, marriage, anointing and funeral rites there
- Consider baptism by immersion for infants and adults to express how we rise to new life in baptism

St Michael's Abbey Church, Farnborough, Hampshire

The *axis mundi* of St Michael's Abbey Church, Farnborough, Hampshire. The abbey church was built by Empress Eugénie, whose tomb is in the crypt with that of her husband, Napoleon III and their son the Prince Imperial, Napoleon IV. The *axis mundi* or pole of the earth is indicated by the medallion of inlaid marble centred under the dome, creating a strong vertical axis that extends to the height of the dome and figuratively to the crypt below, to those awaiting the resurrection of the dead.

The Latin word *suscipio* refers to the act of placing a newborn child at its father's feet. If the father picks it up – *suscipit* – then he assumes responsibility for the child. In monastic profession the monk prostrates in prayer on this central medallion. Next he stands with arms raised and sings, 'Receive (*suscipe*) me, O Lord'. Thus the monk is caught up by God into a share in divine life as a member of the monastic community. The prostration and rising enacts this being caught up. In death the monks lie in state where they professed vows, as they await their rising from the dead.

The altar stands under the triumphal arch of the apse, not in place of the *axis mundi*.

Façade inside and out

14

FROM THERE TO ETERNITY

November is the month when we remember those who have died. It can also be a time to ponder on how the interior and decoration of churches are ordered to reflect on the life hereafter.

Imagine the consoling light when mourners hold lit candles in the darkness as they receive the body of the deceased into church for an all-night vigil. Lighting these candles in the evening is a fitting metaphor for the believer who sleeps in the Lord, and the all-night vigil is a form of waiting with the deceased for the eternal dawn. With the dawning of the new day, the faithful celebrate the eucharistic banquet with rites for the deceased who await the eternal wedding feast of the Lamb. Indeed, lay leaders of funerals may appreciate the gentleness of a candlelit reception of the body into church during Evening Prayer rather than the text-based Liturgy of the Word celebrated as a funeral vigil.

The setting sun provides the occasion for remembering the end of time and eternity beyond. The end of the day was marked by a last bugle call when I was a Boy Scout at summer camp. That same bugle call sounded during my father's graveside service as a final call for his life now at rest.

The setting sun also provides the geography of our passage to eternal life. The Assumption of Mary is often painted on the inside wall of the façade in the Balkan Orthodox tradition.

There it expresses the Christian hope already fulfilled in the God-Bearer. Walking out of such a church, a person walks with the sun towards its setting and sees on the back wall of the assembly hall the image of Mary's Assumption, and then having passed through the façade looks back upon the façade with its heavenly gathering. The façade of Notre Dame Cathedral, Paris, expresses the heavenly company of saints, all facing towards the setting sun. Some parishes have an image of the patron saint, as part of the heavenly company, mounted on the façade facing the setting sun.

Images of the Last Judgement are based on the parable of how Christ will separate the just from the unjust as a shepherd separates the sheep from the goats (Matthew 25.31–46). In this passage, Jesus says he will put the sheep on his right and they shall go to eternal life, but the goats he will put on his left and they shall go to eternal punishment.

This account of the Last Judgement inspired a wall mural called the 'doom' still preserved in a few Norman churches such as All Saints Church, Great Harrowden, Northamptonshire. They were often painted on the inside wall of the façade so that people saw them as they walked out of church. Situated there, the sun would pass over Christ's right shoulder to set beyond, and the sheep would follow. But Christ's left corresponded to the darker regions where the goats were depicted.

Perhaps the most famous example is the *Last Judgement* by Michelangelo on the western wall of the Sistine Chapel. Not unrelated to the doom are the images of Holy Saturday and Easter Sunday in the wall murals of the church at Pickering, in North Yorkshire. There, one image depicts first Christ freeing Adam and Eve and all those waiting for his redemption; another image shows his Resurrection.

Christ separates the sheep from the goats based on one's actions in this life. The just feed the hungry, give drink to the thirsty, shelter the stranger, clothe the naked, care for the sick, visit the imprisoned, and we may add bury the dead. These actions decorate the main doors of the cathedral of Orvieto, Italy, so that as people enter they are reminded of how they have treated their neighbour before presenting their gifts at the altar – and as people exit they are reminded that the way they respond to their neighbour is salvific. Thus, a church's façade functions symbolically as a veil, pierced by a door decorated with emblems of human compassion, because caring for people in their need is a type of passage through which the heavenly reign of God is revealed in daily human encounters.

Churches with a gathering space have another indoor façade at the entrance to the assembly hall. Images on these several walls may narrate the stages of passage into eternity. According to the Byzantine tradition the inner façade typically has an image of the Last Judgement that one would see upon entering the church.

Some churches have numerous sets of doors, and tradition may assign different ritual activities to different doors and to the gathering space or narthex. For example, the community gathers there to form the worshipping body, the Church, and at the end of the service people take their leave as they pass through the façade. Some churches reserve their central doors only for the most solemn occasions. Bridal parties line up in the gathering space and then process through the monumental doors of the inner façade. But the monumental doors of the outer façade are reserved for other ritual actions. There, a bishop knocks on the doors to take possession of the cathedral. These doors are opened especially for bearing the deceased into the church for the funeral liturgies and then for bearing the deceased out towards the setting sun. The main doors serve in this way as a threshold, a gate of passage to eternal life.

Especially on Remembrance Sunday, parish communities might reflect on their rituals of remembering the dead, especially the way they receive the body of a Christian into church and bear the body to its place of rest. They might consider how the ritual actions at the entrance to the church respect these human activities. They might consider the cosmic dimension, that the setting sun provides a time and a geography for considering how they face eternity by facing people this day. Reflecting on the meaning of these rituals may suggest a programme of images and art drawn from the scriptures and personal witness. This artistic programme might narrate the process of our transition from this life to the next, such as the Assumption of Mary, the final judgement based on works of mercy in this life, and the saints in the heavenly company.

To Do

- Imagine the gentle consolation of a candlelit reception of the body into church during Evening Prayer
- Reflect on your rituals of remembering the dead
- Think about how ritual actions at the entrance to the church respect our human activities

St Peter and St Paul Church, Pickering, North Yorkshire

Detail of the fifteenth-century wall murals in St Peter and St Paul Church, Pickering, North Yorkshire. Christ (left) descends among the waiting and grasps Adam's arm to lead him, with Eve following close behind (right) along with all the waiting stepping forth from the mouth of a giant monster that had kept them. Other fanciful beasts can be seen in the background. Adam holds the apple made whole once again, as if to return it. They begin their journey on Christ's left side. Christ's right hand grasps Adam's right arm and leads him with the others presumably to Christ's right side.

Upon entering the church, one can see this image on the right side wall. Thus the image parallels the procession from the front door of church to the altar where the faithful gather at Christ's right side. After the liturgy the faithful make the journey with Christ toward the front door and beyond to encounter the living who are still awaiting their salvation.

While not a scene of the Last Judgement, this image depicts the mystery recalled on Holy Saturday when Christ descended among the dead to free those awaiting his salvation.

Three axes

15

BE GUIDED BY THE LIGHT

From dawn to dusk, the path of the sun throughout the day, as it moves through the church building, can offer a structure for the ritual actions of the liturgy.

Sunlight structures the day from sunrise to midday to sunset. This primary human experience regulates the time of the year and the seasons of growth, the fruitfulness and dormancy of living things. Its daily and annual cycles are a metaphor for the span of human life. Making use of sunlight in a church enhances the experience and more significantly communicates God's encounter with humanity in liturgy.

The English word 'orient' comes from the Latin *oriens* referring to the time, place and action of the rising sun. The midday sun gives its name in Latin, *meridies*, to its time, place and to the midday rest, while the setting sun, *occidens*, gives its name to its time, place and setting. The human experience of daybreak, the midday heat and sunset are prior to abstractions such as the cardinal directions east, south, west. Only the north is not named according to the sun in Latin.

Sunlight animates place and structures three-dimensional space; light structures human action in time and place. A clock turning clockwise mimics the rotation of the shadow on a sundial in the northern hemisphere. Native peoples of the North American plains call this direction of rotation 'sunwise', which expresses the primary human experience of the sun's move-ment across the landscape, more so than does 'clockwise'. They dance sunwise around the drum and move sunwise within a tipi, because such respects the natural order; to move otherwise portents calamity.

Sunwise also describes the ever-changing architecture of light moving through a church and suggests a structure for the ritual actions of liturgy and a programme for the art and architecture. Providing a window in the apse of a church allows the first light of dawn to appear. The Gospel Canticle at Morning Prayer acclaims of Christ: 'the dawn from on high will break upon us, to give light to those who sit in darkness and in the shadow of death, to guide our feet into the way of peace' (Luke 1.78–79, *NRSV*). Christ is the dawn, not its abstraction, the east.

This light shining through the apse offers a metaphor for the three-fold coming of Christ. He came first in the humility of the babe lying in the manger, he comes in the Word and banquet, and he will come again in glory. A parish could depict the Incar-nation in the apse, illuminated by the light of dawn. The light of daybreak shining into the church suggests a ritual direction for Christ's coming when the book of the Gospels and his body and blood are carried from the altar to encounter the faithful.

Christ comes as a light to guide one's feet on the way, sug-gesting another procession of the faithful coming towards the morning light to meet Christ and share Communion. This double procession of Christ coming with the dawn from the altar toward the faithful, themselves entering through the main doors and processing towards the light, towards the altar, establishes the main axis of the church from altar to door, from daybreak to sunset. Light, words, actions reinforce this personal encounter of Christ and his body, the Church.

The procession toward the sun suggests that we pray and walk sunward. The main axes of early basilicas in Rome face any which way, except with the apse facing due east. In several basilicas such as St Peter's, the presider standing at the altar faces toward the sunrise, but in others toward the sun at some point in the day, more rightly called sunward, *ad lucem*, rather than *ad orientem*, toward sunrise.

As daybreak offers its metaphor for the Incarnation, the setting sun completes this axis, suggesting the end of time when Christ will come again in majesty to judge based on whether a person fed the hungry, gave drink to the thirsty, sheltered the stranger, clothed the naked, cared for the sick, visited the imprisoned (Matthew 25.31–46). A parish could revive the tradition of decorating the back wall of the church with the judgement scene, and the central doors of the church with images of these corporal works of mercy, including burying the dead.

The sun reaches its climax at midday, when it stands not directly overhead but to the side so that its rays shine across the church, as at St Michael's Abbey, Farnborough, depicted on page xxxvi of this book. Westminster Cathedral follows the tradition of placing the ambo on the midday side of the nave so that the maximum luminosity of the sun shines from behind the deacon, who faces with the sun's rays crossing the church to proclaim the Gospel. The side of the midday sun is chosen for the ambo, as the monument of the empty tomb, so that maximum sunlight crossing the church may provide a cosmic metaphor for the Resurrection, in whose light all scripture is interpreted.

The height of the midday sun establishes the third axis of a church – following the first axis from daybreak to sunset with the double procession from altar and door to the divine encounter, and the second axis of the midday sun shining across the church with the proclamation of scripture from ambo's empty tomb.

This third axis is often expressed by a dome or a crossing. A good example is the Anglican, St Paul's Cathedral, London, where the height of the dome is echoed in the design of the floor pavement, suggesting that the floor extends downward to the nether reaches where Christ journeyed to claim those awaiting him. From there, he ascended to sit at the right hand of God on high. The centre design of that pavement is a starburst, and anyone who stands on it is, as it were, suspended between the depths and the heights and is caught up in Christ's ascent. At such a place, weddings, religious professions, ordinations, anointings and funerals are suitably celebrated.

The renovation of the Crystal Cathedral in Garden Grove, California, now becoming Christ Cathedral, provides an opportunity to arrange the building and the processions so that the ever-changing light will animate the interior arrangement, nuance the ritual narrative and structure the programme of art.

If space and light are used well in a church, the personal experience of the sun from daybreak to sunset, from midday across the church and from the shades below to the sun's zenith, can each be a metaphor for Christ the light.

To Do

- Be aware of the natural lighting in the church and use more of it
- Invite people to reflect on the double procession as being symbolic of the reciprocal relationship between Christ and themselves
- Consider the course of the sun when you build or renovate a church

Basilica of Santa Maria in Cosmedin, *Rome*

The Basilica of *Santa Maria in Cosmedin*, Rome. Abbot Desiderius of Monte Cassino (later Pope Victor III, 1086–87) invited artisans from Constantinople to renovate the Abbey. One of the artisan skills he attracted was the mosaic work best known for the Cosmati family. Accordingly this diaconal church was renovated and the ambo installed between 1118 and 1124.

All the axes and dimensions are well developed in this church. The main axis leads from the door to the altar and ciborium. On the left the ambo enclosure has a balcony for proclaiming the epistle and on the right the monument of the empty tomb from which the deacon proclaims the Gospel while facing across the church with the rays of the midday sun. The spiral column is the Easter candleholder. Between the ambo and altar a beam bisects the church into two parts, the near side for the Liturgy of the Word at the ambo and chairs and the far side for the Eucharistic Liturgy at the altar. The presidential chair is at the head of the apse with a bench along the apse wall for the presbyters.

This and San Clemente's ambos have enclosures, but Westminster Cathedral's ambo is free standing.

Ministry of presiding from the chair

16

IT'S THE TAKING PART

Christ is present in the celebration of the Eucharist and the Holy Spirit prompts the assembly to respond. A deeper involvement by the whole congregation will help people to discern this.

The renewal of the Eucharist beginning with that of the Easter vigil in 1951 and continuing both before and after the Second Vatican Council has enhanced an appreciation of the particular ministry of the priest and the active participation of the whole people of God. As in life, there is a certain mutuality in celebrating well.

Presiding well at the liturgy involves promoting and fostering others and uniting everyone. When people know that they are valued and their contribution appreciated, the whole dynamic of presiding at the liturgy changes. When Pope John Paul II dedicated the Mother of the Redeemer Chapel in the papal apartments, he stood at his chair and handed the lectionary to a woman who received it, and then she proclaimed one of the scripture readings, while the Pope and all present were seated and listened.

Simple gestures made at the chair suggest the two sides of presiding at the liturgy: confirming the ministry of others and receiving their ministry. In giving the lectionary, the Pope entrusted the woman with proclaming the Word of God and then he and all present sat down to recognize and receive Christ present in the scripture she proclaimed. Imitating this papal example promotes the good celebration of the Sunday Eucharist. The presider, like the Pope, is to confirm the contribution of others to the liturgy and to recognize Christ present in their lives and contribution.

Christ is present, for example, in the scriptures proclaimed as well as in the life of the baptized person proclaiming the readings. It is important that lectors realize that the words they proclaim are the word of the Lord, heard and received as Christ present. When Christ is present in the word proclaimed, the Spirit prompts the faithful to respond personally by giving themselves. A brief pause after the first reading provides an opportunity for everyone to reflect on the word of God just proclaimed and to consider their personal response before the communal response is given with the help of the cantor, choir and musicians when all sing the responsorial psalm. The musicians, then, help everyone yield to the promptings of the Spirit in response to Christ present; it is not their task to respond in the place of everyone else. Indeed, musicians, lectors and presiders may act with such eagerness that they disregard the most essential elements, that Christ is present in his body, the Church, and that the Spirit prompts Christians to respond to Christ present.

Liturgical responses are part of the personal cooperation with the Spirit at work in the members of the assembly urging them to respond to Christ present. The presider sets an example through discernment of the various ways Christ reveals himself and sensitivity to the Spirit prompting each person to respond. Lectors too may be more responsive by proclaiming the Word of God in such a way that people are able to receive it as Christ present and with such patience as permits people to respond as the Spirit prompts. Proclaiming is not just about reading a text out loud, but involves a rapport with the listener.

Musicians likewise may more consciously place their gift at

the service of the Spirit who is already at work in the faithful, prompting them to respond, and then support their response in song.

This sequence is especially evident at the Easter vigil when each reading is followed by a psalm or canticle sung by all, and these are concluded by a prayer given from the presidential chair. This suggests that leading the prayer be added to confirming and receiving the ministry of others. Leading the prayer is much more than simply reciting the assigned text from the book, as if it were the only prayer offered in church. Leading the prayer includes, first, an invitation to pray followed by sufficient silence so that all present have the opportunity to formulate and offer their personal prayer. Respecting this silence for personal prayer is not easy, especially in larger groups of people.

In many parishes, this pause lasts only long enough for the server to position the book for the presider to read the prayer. I have asked people how long it takes them to consider, compose and offer a personal prayer, and next I asked them to do so in the amount of time they stipulated. They often underestimate by far the amount of time they actually need, and even more time is needed for a large gathering of people to do the same. Leading the prayer also involves reciting the assigned prayer in such a way that all present may make it their own in the hearing, and give their assent, 'Amen'.

Leading others in this prayer is more than simply saying it for them; it involves respecting others in this communal process of shared prayer. The root meaning of both the verb 'to preside' and the noun 'president' comes from a Latin expression meaning 'to sit before', but presiding in the liturgical assembly is different from, for example, conducting a committee meeting. The ministry of presiding is summarized briefly in the introduction to the Roman Missal: 'The chair of the Priest Celebrant must signify his function of presiding over the gathering and of directing the prayer' (translation by author, *GIRM*, 310).

For the first time in centuries the priest was instructed to sit down and listen to the scriptures proclaimed by another only since the reform of the Easter vigil by Pius XII beginning in 1951. This initial renewal of the Easter vigil presaged the renewal of the liturgy after the Second Vatican Council. The model used for the renewed order of the Eucharist was the solemn celebration at which a bishop presides and in which the richly ministerial nature of the people of God is fully expressed in the variety of ordered ministries. One of the tasks of the presider, then, is to nurture others in developing their awareness of and contribution to the communal celebration.

Many people emphasize that the priest acts in the person of Christ; this describes the priest's status. But the ministry of presiding at the liturgy and directing the prayer concerns helping the faithful to recognize Christ present in the people gathered celebrating the liturgy, in the Word proclaimed, in the meal shared and in the Church sent to be Christ to the world, and to recognize the Spirit's prompting the people gathered to give themselves to Christ manifested in their midst.

To Do

- Presiders: be attentive to others
- Other ministers: be mindful that Christ is present through you and the Spirit is at work
- All the baptized: consider how the Spirit prompts you to bring Christ's presence to others

Cathedral of St Anne, Leeds, West Yorkshire

The altar and cathedra of the Cathedral of St Anne, Leeds, West Yorkshire. The traditional arrangement for the bishop's chair, called a cathedra, is preserved at the head of the assembly in this recently renovated cathedral. The bishop's chair sits on a small platform raised six steps higher than the altar. A heightened medieval example is found in Norwich Cathedral.

The chair is a place of prayer and of presiding. At this chair the bishop affirms the ministries of others and then receives their ministry, as when the bishop sits to listen to the scripture proclaimed by the lector or stands while the deacon proclaims the Gospel, and then sits down to teach the local church from the chair.

St Augustine of Hippo said that his chair was elevated in the apse of the church so that as a bishop he might oversee the liturgical assembly, yet as a brother he stood with all the baptized. Church ruins in North Africa preserve the early practice of placing the altar in the midst of the nave, as once was the case in the Basilicas of St Mary Major and St Mary in Trastevere, Rome. The Blessed Sacrament is reserved here in its own worthy chapel.

17

THRESHOLD OF
TRANSCENDENCE

An encounter with God may be perceived not only at church through the liturgy but also through the rich symbolism of the building itself. Understanding the architecture can enhance Christians' life of faith.

Christianity is a very 'fleshy' religion. That, of course, is due to having an incarnate God at its heart, but it is also because it has a profound understanding that all human experience of transcendence is mediated through the body. Both the encounter with the Transcendent God and the personal process of transcending one's former self and coming to a new identity are mediated bodily.

Take, for example, baptism. A person professes faith with his or her lips and is washed in water and so comes to know himself or herself as a child of God. In Confirmation, a person receives the laying-on of hands and is anointed with oil and so is anointed with the Spirit of God. In the Eucharist, Christians share Communion by eating from a common loaf and drinking from a common cup and so share Communion with one another in the body and blood of Christ.

Many transitions take place in a person's life, such as starting school, marriage and childbirth. In each experience, a person transcends his or her former self and comes to a new identity in an ever-enlarging social context with an ever greater capacity for intimacy.

People develop personal depth and breadth, particular and universal humanity through experiences of self-transcendence. Preparation for adult baptism is less concerned with doctrinal instruction than with sharing faith and nurturing a relationship with the Triune God. Benedictine monks profess a vow of stability that anchors them in a particular community from which they serve the larger church. The Little Sisters of Jesus, in contrast, follow an international formation whereby the newly professed are uprooted from their immediate neighbourhood and even their country. Then they are assigned to serve the vulnerable in another culture so that the sister may discover their common humanity in communion with those around them. A church building supports well-developed ritual expressions of the transcendent capacity of the human person and the encounter with the Transcendent God.

Crossing the threshold helps us realize what transcendence means: the entrance into a church may pass through a baptistery, as at Corpus Christi parish, Lawrence, Kansas, where the font is surrounded by eight pillars supporting a dome. A person crosses a threshold from the gathering area to enter into the baptistery. The water-bath and skylight above suggest coming to new life in baptism and personal illumination. They cross another threshold when they pass into the hall or nave of the church.

In the hall or nave, the Word of God is proclaimed, and the communal response incorporates scripture, reflection and prayer. The sound echoes in the hall, and then dissipates; but the Word takes lasting root in each person. This Word pierces the heart and moves the community to do the work of God in the world. The transition from the nave to the eucharistic table in some old churches such as *San Clemente* and *Santa Sabina*, Rome, is indicated by a low wall that separates the Liturgy of the Word on the nave side from the Eucharistic Liturgy celebrated in the apse. A later development is seen at *Santa Maria in Cosmedin*, Rome, where this low wall supports pillars holding a marble beam that extends all the way across the nave, bisecting the church and distinguishing the Liturgy of the Word from the Eucharistic Liturgy. The practice of hanging icons from the upper beam eventually was to develop into the icon wall or iconostasis prominent in some churches.

This transition is also marked by the rood screen. Some are monumental stone structures, such as the one at Lincoln Cathedral, which may have once incorporated a place in the upper level for the proclamation of the Gospel. Others are a light wooden lattice as at Our Lady St Mary, South Creake, Norfolk, where the wall nearby still contains a stairwell perhaps giving similar access to the upper level of a larger, but no longer extant rood screen. A triumphal arch indicates this in some churches, as at Ealing Abbey, London.

Such a threshold need not separate people from clergy. At Mother of the Church Convent near Rugby, a line in the floor indicates this passage, which is crossed to receive Communion. At Douai Abbey, Berkshire, guests join the monks in the choir for the weekday Liturgy of the Word, and then all process under a suspended cross and gather around the altar for the Eucharistic Liturgy, as they do also at New Camaldoli Hermitage, Big Sur, California.

This threshold marks a passage to greater intimacy in Communion around the table of the Lord. When people bring the bread and wine all the way to the altar, they all the more clearly indicate that they are also presenting themselves with the gifts. The divine gift given in response is the Holy Spirit brooding over the gifts as represented on the baldachin or ciborium above the altar. As the morning dew forms on the grass, so the Spirit makes the gifts holy and unites the community into one so that they may accomplish the divine work in the world.

Christians share Communion with one another in the body and blood of Christ. Augustine of Hippo (354–430), speaking in the voice of Christ, says of Communion: 'You will not change me into you like the food of your flesh, but you will be changed into me' (translation by author, *Confessions*, Book VII, chapter 10, para. 16). Cyril of Jerusalem (c. 315–386) compares Communion to an infant nursing at the breast in the nuptial chamber. To this, I suggest that, as Christians mature to become adult daughters and sons of God, they are called to enter the same bridal chamber now as spouse. After being renewed by this greater intimacy with God and with others through Communion, Christians are then sent out from the Lord's table. The symbolic journey made towards God is now repeated in reverse: they once again cross each threshold, which now opens up to a broader social world. They pass by the font to bless themselves with its water as they go out to live their baptismal calling in daily life.

Participating in liturgy – including understanding the way in which the architectural space of churches expresses our connection with God – teaches a transcendent way of life in which a person's every action, whether writing, preparing to teach or sharing food and drink with another, is to be done with an openness to God, to oneself and to others. Helping parishioners understand the richness of their own church's symbolism will in turn strengthen their fellowship with God.

To Do

- Ask people to bring the bread and wine all the way to the altar and so present themselves as gift
- Bless yourself with baptismal water as you leave Mass
- Use the building itself to deepen the parish's faith

Church of Our Lady St Mary, South Creake, Norfolk

The rood screen at the Church of Our Lady St Mary, South Creake, Norfolk. The old altar is under the sunrise window (left), and the sunset window illuminates the baptistery at the entrance. The sun establishes the double procession as Christ comes in word and sacrament like the daybreak from on high and the baptized come to meet him.

The distinction between the Liturgy of the Word and the Eucharistic Liturgy is beautifully expressed by this rood screen, which was more substantial when a spiral staircase opened onto its no longer extant balcony. The staircase is on the side of the midday sun so that the deacon could proclaim the Gospel facing with the sun's rays shining across the church, as an English development of the ambo.

Liturgical activity is like a veil that reveals fundamental values and truths by which we live and mature throughout our lives. So too the latticework of this rood screen provides a veil that reveals and so beckons us to pass beyond by sharing the Eucharistic meal. This architectural distinction expresses the processional nature of liturgy, especially where the whole assembly processes from the place of the word to the place of the Eucharist.

III

FIVE WAYS TO ARRANGE
A CHURCH

Standing around the altar

18

GATHER THEM IN

The altar has a central focus in liturgical life, which need not be lost if it is moved from the centre point of the church. Placing an altar off-centre can open up a more dynamic participation in a range of ritual practices.

Many recently built or renovated churches have an altar in the geographic centre of the crossing, directly under the dome or in the centre of the people; but for all its benefits, this position flattens the celebration of liturgy and stands in contrast to the examples of early churches.

Many people presume that the altar at St Peter's Basilica in Rome is centred under the dome, but it is set slightly behind centre so that an imaginary vertical line extending from the centre of the dome passes just in front of the baldachin and altar and down into the lower level where the tomb of the Apostle is visible. Setting this altar back allows the vertical axis to develop a focus on the apostolic tomb in this mortuary basilica.

In contrast, since the Second Vatican Council many altars have been relocated from the far end of a long hall to a geographic centre of the building so that people may gather around it. One motive for this was found in the text of the early Roman Eucharistic Prayer, now number 1: *Memento … omnium circumstantium*, meaning exactly, 'Be mindful … of all [people] standing around' as in, standing in a circle (*MR 2008*, translation by author). This has been rendered in the new translation without reference to standing (*stantium*) nor to 'around' (*circum*) in the still accurate expression, 'Remember ... all gathered here'.

This phrase of the prayer was often promoted at the time of Vatican II by those who wanted the faithful to stand around a central altar so that they would be able to participate better in the liturgy by seeing the actions at the altar and hearing the prayers. Such arrangements provide immediate rapport with the altar and thus enhance the participation of people in the liturgy. People who are drawn into a more immediate contact with one another standing around a central altar may be prompted to assume greater responsibility for the practice of their faith in regard to their neighbour and their liturgical participation.

But such a central arrangement comes at the cost of diminishing other aspects of the liturgical life of a parish. For example, when the altar occupies the vertical axis, these two dimensions are conflated into one, thereby diminishing ritual possibilities. But when the vertical axis stands free, as at St Peter's Basilica, it allows a secondary focus. In a parish it may serve as a place of ritual activity such as receiving Communion and anointings, the exchange of marriage vows, religious professions and ordinations, a place of rest for the deceased during a funeral vigil and liturgy.

When these two axes are more fully developed, the baldachin or ciborium over the altar expresses the gift of the Spirit upon the bread and wine placed on the altar, just as the dome expresses the gift of the Spirit descending upon the body of Christ, the Church, often gathered under an image of Christ the Lord of All located at the centre of the dome's ceiling. Sadly, this symbolic meaning of the dome is displaced from the body of Christ, the Church, to the altar when centred below without its own proper baldachin or ciborium.

When the altar is in the centre of a circle, the processional character of the liturgy is diminished because all movement is in relation to this one point. A procession can move in and out or around the circle, but the central focus does not allow for different places for processions to and from. A central altar produces a more static liturgy. When the altar occupies the only focus of a building, the Liturgy of the Word does not have its own natural architectural space and is thereby diminished even though the development of the Liturgy of the Word, along with the cycle of scripture readings, is one of the hallmarks of the liturgical reform following the council.

The rich ministerial character of the liturgy is diminished when areas of liturgical activity are not well developed other than the altar which focuses on the ministry of the ordained. The centrality of the altar in the liturgical life of a parish and the more immediate participation it engenders need not be lost if the altar is moved away from the central focus so that a fuller arrangement may be developed that provides several different foci for different liturgical ministries.

The altar can reclaim its position as the goal of a processional way without locating it at the extreme end of a long hall. Recent excavation has revealed a worthy example in one of the first central plan churches built in Rome, St Stephen in the Round. Presently, the altar stands on a raised platform in the centre point of the circular structure. But, in the original arrangement, the altar stood at the edge of the central drum at the end of a processional way. Thus, the processional way was combined with the intimacy and participation of a central plan that left the vertical axis free for other ritual activity and an ample space and focus for the celebration of the Liturgy of the Word.

A different solution was developed at Rome's cathedral, the Lateran, and at St Paul's Outside the Walls. The floor plan of each basilica is a variant on the shape of a cross, but the altar is not located at the centre of the crossing, nor is it set back into the apse. Rather, these altars, establishing subsequent Roman practice, are situated forward towards the front door so that they stand at the head of the nave, just beyond the triumphal arch into the transept. Thus, the centre of the crossing is open and the transept is available for seating all the way around the altar when needed.

Members of a parish building or renovation committee may find inspiration in these several arrangements that preserve the strong sense of communion among the people gathered around a central altar and of participation in the liturgy celebrated together, while maintaining the procession along an axis to and from the altar. These examples also inspire more fully developed architectural arrangements for the celebration of the Liturgy of the Word and the rites that naturally occur at the vertical axis when intentionally left empty and so available for people.

A parish need not renovate its church, however, to consider how it already uses the space available and how it might develop these places for a fuller celebration of all the rituals of a parish community.

To Do

- Invite people into more immediate contact with one another around the altar
- Develop places for a fuller celebration of all the rituals of your parish community
- Encourage people to practise greater participation in liturgy and charity towards their neighbour

Sacred Heart Chapel of St Benedict's Monastery, St Joseph, Minnesota

Sacred Heart Chapel of St Benedict's Monastery, St Joseph, Minnesota. The Benedictine sisters' chapel is cruciform, with seating on all four sides of the central altar occupying the sole focus of the crossing. The lectern (left) and presider's chair (right) are in secondary places on the platform on opposite sides of the altar along an axis formed by the transept, thus utilizing both the long processional axis and the shorter transept axis in different ways.

St Peter's Basilica, the Lateran and St Paul's Outside the Walls suggest alternatives to this central altar arrangement. If this altar were moved off-centre and given its own closely tailored platform, as in those basilicas, the central platform could be levelled so that its marble outline would provide the frame for an *axis mundi* where sisters could make their profession, receive Communion, receive blessings and anointings and rest during their funeral liturgy in the place where they professed their vows.

If an ambo were provided as a monument of the empty tomb, the example of the myrrh-bearing women telling the Good News to the disciples would provide a narrative for the sisters to tell their own story from the very place where the scriptures are proclaimed.

19

TABLE OF GOOD
CONTENTS

There are two forms of nourishment at Mass: that of the
Eucharist and that of scripture readings. But they are different
ways of feeding the person. The style of delivery, design of
the church and references in homilies can point to scripture's
unique contribution.

Christians are nourished at the table of the Word of God better
now than ever before, but the limits of the metaphor 'table of the
Word' are surpassed by Jesus' example in his inaugural address
at the synagogue in Nazareth.

The revision of the cycle of readings after the Second Vatican
Council was so successful that it immediately became a point
of ecumenical convergence. Today, most churches that follow a
regular cycle of readings proclaim, hear, reflect on and pray from
the same Gospel passages and other scriptural readings on most
Sundays. Homilies, then, focus on practically the same readings
from scripture. This all was inspired by people who spoke during
Vatican II in favour of being nourished more fully at the table of
the Word as at the eucharistic table.

In this light, the architectural design of a number of churches
constructed or renovated since the council includes a table where
the Eucharist is celebrated and a smaller version of the same table

design used as a 'table of the Word' with a book-holder on it. In some churches the two tables are placed together in a sanctuary at the end of the central aisle, in others they are arranged along the central aisle itself, and the seating on both sides is arranged facing this centre aisle.

One of the benefits of the latter arrangement is that no one has to look down a long church to a distant sanctuary; they can look across the aisle and see their neighbours, as together they turn their attention first to the table of the Word and then to the eucharistic table. Such an arrangement manifests architecturally the two parts of the liturgy – Word and sacrament – that together form 'one single act of worship' as the Vatican II *Constitution on the Sacred Liturgy* puts it (article 56, *DEC*).

The difficulty with this arrangement was noted by several participants at the council who pointed out that these two are not tables in the same way and thus form an unequal pairing. The eucharistic table is a banquet table at which the Church celebrates the Lord's Supper; the table of the Word, however, is a metaphorical table. The benefit of manifesting architecturally the two parts of the liturgy as two tables also has the disadvantage of recasting the proclamation of the Word of God in the light of the eucharistic banquet, rather than according to its own ritual and architectural arrangement.

But the ritual of the eucharistic table cannot be recast for the table of the Word. As Jesus took bread and wine, the people of God bring bread and wine to the eucharistic table. As Jesus blessed them and gave thanks, the assembly, in union with the Church, gives thanks to God over the gifts. As Jesus broke the bread and shed his blood, the minister breaks the bread, and the wine is poured. And, as Jesus gave his body and blood, the Church shares in this Communion.

The proclamation of the Good News has to follow a different ritual structure, one followed by Jesus in his inaugural address. Returning from the desert, he entered the synagogue at Nazareth

99

and stood to read from the scroll of the book of Isaiah. When he had finished, 'he rolled up the scroll, gave it back to the attendant, and sat down. The eyes of all ... were fixed on him. Then he began to say to them, "Today this scripture has been fulfilled in your hearing"' (Luke 4.21, *NRSV*).

As Jesus stood to proclaim the scripture, the lector stands and the entire assembly stands for the Gospel. As Jesus had the scroll put away, the lectionary should be put away after the proclamation. As Jesus sat down to teach, bishops teach while seated in the chair. Other presiders could likewise give the homily from the chair, where they ideally remain while the deacon proclaims the Gospel. There was a pregnant pause before Jesus started to speak, just as today people need a moment to reflect. Jesus said that the words of the prophet were fulfilled in him. Likewise, the current readings are selected in such a way that the first reading, typically from the Old Testament, foreshadows its fulfilment in the Gospel. One task of the homily is to point to this fulfilment in Christ.

No image better captures the fulfilment of all things in Christ than the angel at the empty tomb announcing that he is risen, 'go quickly and tell his disciples' (Matthew 28.7, *NRSV*). The astonished women ran to tell the Good News both in word and in its effect on them personally. Evangelizing has vitality when this Good News is proclaimed both in word and in one's life. From this, there developed the tradition of designing an empty tomb from which the Alleluia is sung and the Gospel proclaimed. For example, at Westminster Cathedral on solemn occasions, the Gospel is proclaimed from the platform on the right side of the nave raised on columns with an empty space below, as if proclaiming the Good News from the empty tomb; there, a medallion of the victorious lamb that was slain is the positive expression of Christ's victory over death.

These actions of Jesus are also seen in the monastic practice of 'holy reading', *lectio divina*. This practice begins with reading the scripture aloud, followed by a moment of silence which allows for personal reflection. Next, a personal response is given in prayer, and the entire process culminates in moments of appreciating the insight. This practice structures the Liturgy of the Word. After the first reading, there is to be a moment of silence for personal reflection. The community responds to this reading through the responsorial psalm. Then the process begins again with the second reading and the Gospel. All of this is followed by a shared reflection in the homily and leads to the prayers of the faithful. Throughout this process, people come to their own moments of appreciating insights as the Spirit prompts.

Jesus' inaugural address provides the structure for the Liturgy of the Word just as his actions at the Last Supper provide the structure for the Eucharistic Liturgy. The eucharistic banquet complements the Liturgy of the Word, whose proper symbolic architecture in the empty tomb supports the ritual proclamation of a richer fare of sripture and response, fulfilled in Christ.

To Do

- Include moments of silent reflection after each reading
- Focus homilies on the day's scripture
- Consider rearranging the seating in your church so that people face the centre aisle

Choir chapel of Mount St Scholastica Monastery, Atchison, Kansas

The choir chapel of Mount St Scholastica Monastery, Atchison, Kansas. The antiphonal seating has choir stalls on both sides facing the centre aisle. The high-backed altar no longer used, the new altar was made of white marble in the form of a table. A smaller version of that table was developed as a table of the Word (foreground) from which the scriptures are proclaimed. The two-part structure of the liturgy is well represented by two distinct places of celebration in this successful example of the two-table arrangement.

The eucharistic table functions as a table for the Lord's Supper, but the table of the Word functions only metaphorically as a table. Rather than force the table imagery proper to a banquet onto the place of proclaiming the scripture, one could create an ambo according to its own proper symbolic structure as a monument of the empty tomb and situate it in the same place as the table of the Word.

The sisters might recount their own ministry at such a monument of the empty tomb in terms of the myrrh-bearing women who came sorrowful to anoint Jesus' body, but the angel commanded them to go and tell the Good News to the disciples.

Two-part structure of the Eucharist

20

STAND UP FOR THE LORD

The two parts of the Mass – the Liturgy of the Word and Liturgy of the Eucharist – are both distinct and at the same time deeply interconnected. The altar, chair and ambo should be arranged if possible to help make this overall liturgical structure more intelligible.

The table of the Lord has no chair. No one sits at this table, so a chair is not needed there. Instead, according to ancient custom, the presiding priest stands to offer the Eucharistic Prayer and everyone stands at least for parts of the rite. Early Eucharistic Prayers speak of standing around the altar or of standing at the altar before the Lord, and these are preserved in the Latin texts of current Eucharistic Prayers.

In the fourteenth-century Renaissance, the distinct place for the proclamation of scripture at the ambo was removed in many churches to free the space from 'medieval' accretions. Thereafter the altar came to predominate as the exclusive place for the readings as well as the Eucharist. Before Pope Pius XII began the reform of the Easter Vigil in 1951, the priest used to read all of the Vigil's 12 readings at the altar; with this reform, for the first time in centuries, the priest was instructed to sit down and listen to the lector proclaiming the scriptures.

To assist in implementing the Vatican II *Constitution on the Sacred Liturgy*, Pope Paul VI established a group known as the *Consilium*. The chief task of the Consilium was to produce reformed liturgical texts and to facilitate the full, conscious and active participation of the people of God in the celebration of the liturgy. This participation would be easier, they reasoned, if the structure of the Mass were evident.

So, in developing the Order of Mass, the Consilium used the solemn papal liturgy as a basis to establish that each of the two parts of the Mass be celebrated in distinct places: first, the Liturgy of the Word at both the ambo and the chairs; and second, the Eucharistic Liturgy at the altar. This two-part structure appears in the *General Instruction of the Roman Missal*: 'The Mass consists in some sense of two parts, namely the Liturgy of the Word and the Liturgy of the Eucharist, these being so closely interconnected that they form but one single act of worship' (*GIRM*, 28; see: *Constitution on the Sacred Liturgy*, 56).

In many churches built after the Second Vatican Council, all three pieces of furniture – lectern, chair, altar – are grouped together without distinguishing between the two places of celebration.

Typically in sanctuaries the altar is centred on a platform and is flanked by the lectern and chair. This is so especially in fan-shaped churches centring on what architects call a 'centre-thrust stage'. The designer Frank Kacmarcik, working from Minnesota, preferred to centre the chair behind the altar and lectern, with the altar placed in front but to one side and the lectern to the other. A more recent adaptation is the 'liturgical peninsula', an elongated platform extending into the midst of the seating; the altar, lectern and chair are lined up on the peninsula fore and aft. When the two parts of the Mass are not well distinguished, the ritual and especially the processions are less developed, and the overall structure of the liturgy is less intelligible.

This distinction was evident at St Peter's Basilica when Pope Benedict sat in a chair on the left side of the nave against the last pier before the central dome. He sat facing across the nave towards the statue of St Peter, opposite. On these occasions a lectern was placed in front of the statue so that, as the Pope sat to listen to the scriptures proclaimed by the lector, they faced one another. The chair and lectern as a pair are distinct but not separated from the altar standing on its own dais raised over the tomb of the Apostle.

This papal practice is more fully developed in the cathedral at Trapani, Sicily, where the bishop's chair, the cathedra, likewise is placed on the left side of the nave against the last pillar before the central dome. It faces across the nave towards a monumental ambo erected on the nave's right side under the last arch before the crossing. There the Liturgy of the Word is celebrated at the bishop's cathedra and the ambo. For the Eucharistic Liturgy, the bishop and ministers process to the apse where they stand at the altar.

The Mother of the Redeemer Chapel in the papal apartments at the Vatican was renovated in 1999 in honour of Pope John Paul II's sixtieth anniversary of ordination. That squarish room was arranged with chairs on two sides facing a centre aisle. In the centre of the aisle is a lectern that faces the Pope's chair located at one end of the aisle. The Liturgy of the Word is celebrated at lectern and chair, before the ministers process to the opposite end of the aisle to stand around the altar for the Eucharistic Liturgy.

Similarly, at my monastery in Atchison, Kansas, guests are welcomed into the monastic choir, where the presidential chair and lectern are placed in the centre aisle facing one another for weekday liturgies. After the Liturgy of the Word, the presider and ministers process to the altar for the Eucharistic Liturgy.

This papal practice is further developed at Douai Abbey, Berkshire, where guests join the monks in choir for the weekday Liturgy of the Word, after which everyone processes to the altar for the Eucharistic Liturgy. At Big Sur, California, the monastic community celebrates the Liturgy of the Word in a dedicated space with chairs and ambo, and then for the Lord's Supper everyone processes to stand around the altar in its dedicated space.

Many medieval parish churches in England have a rood or chancel screen that serves to distinguish between the two parts of the liturgy. A good example is the Church of England parish at Salle, Norfolk, where the presidential chair sits on the left side of the nave against the last pillar and faces across the nave directly towards the triple pulpit. The Liturgy of the Word is celebrated there, after which the procession enters the apse through a gate in a low wall, in lieu of a chancel or rood screen, and the eucharistic part is celebrated at the altar.

A community may consider adapting the arrangement of its church or chapel so that the presidential chair is distinguished among the seating so arranged for all to listen to the proclamation of the scriptures, and then the ministers or even everyone process to the altar for the Eucharistic Liturgy.

To Do

- Discuss with others in your parish how you distinguish between the Liturgy of the Word and the Eucharistic Liturgy
- Consider adapting the arrangement of your church to support this distinction in the way you pair the lectern and chair distinct from the altar
- Develop the processions and the ritual in your parish to increase awareness of the overall structure of the liturgy

The omphalos *of Stanbrook Abbey Church,
North Yorkshire England*

When the abbey relocated from Stanbrook in Worcester to Wass in North Yorkshire, they brought these tiles from the previous church and inlaid them into the floor of their new church. The tiles establish an *omphalos* or 'navel', also called an *axis mundi* or 'pole of the world', which marks the place of the sisters' own transformation and sharing in divine life. Here the sisters prostrate and then rise to make their monastic profession, and once again they lie here in death while the community keeps vigil through the night until the morning Eucharist, as the deceased await their rising to share in the heavenly banquet.

These tiles are located at the intersection of two axes of the abbey church that cross unusually at a 30° angle. One axis runs from the sisters' entrance, past a bowl of baptismal water, between the choir stalls to the altar and beyond to the Blessed Sacrament chapel. This is the Liturgical axis for recalling baptism and celebrating Eucharist, anointing's and daily prayer. The other axis extends from the guests' entrance in one corner and runs diagonally across the chapel to the opposite corner where an off-centre apse accommodates monastic rituals.

The tiles say:

+ *in omnibus glorificetur deus*
+ *et arduis pax et amor*

which means in English:

+ in all things may God be glorified
+ both peace and love in difficulties

Basilica tradition

A PLACE FOR EVERYONE

The internal arrangement of a church speaks of how the Eucharist and other sacraments are celebrated and how the Gospel is proclaimed – and important lessons can be learned from the past.

The basilica of St John Lateran, Rome's cathedral, does not have a sanctuary in the current sense of the word, nor does the basilica of St Paul Outside the Walls. These basilicas follow an earlier Roman practice, where the altar is free-standing on its own platform of several steps. The steps are narrowly limited by the four pillars of the baldachin or ciborium arching over the altar. The only place for ministers to stand on this platform is at the back of the altar, facing the people.

Visitors to the Lateran and St Paul's Outside the Walls can approach very close to these altars because the steps around them are closely circumscribed, giving the altars a sense of immediacy, even intimacy, despite their grandeur. St Peter's Basilica is similar, but, when the bishop presides, a platform is typically erected that bridges over the *confessio* – the opening in the floor in front of the altar to the lower level for venerating the tomb of St Peter. A chair for the bishop is placed on this platform. Without such a platform, no one can stand on the front side of these altars, because one would fall into the *confessio*.

The situation is different in many parishes. Before the liturgical renewal mandated by the Second Vatican Council, many parishes had an altar built against the back wall of a large sanctuary bordered by an altar rail. The scripture readings were read by the priest at the altar in Latin. Leading up to the council, the scripture was more frequently read also in the vernacular from a lectern facing the people from within the sanctuary. Some churches had a pulpit in the nave for preaching.

During Vatican II, many bishops expressed a strong desire to face the people both from the altar and during the readings. Many parish communities constructed a second, free-standing altar facing the people, just as the bishop of Rome has always done in the major basilicas. Some parish communities wanted to bring the altar into closer contact with the people, so they removed the altar rail and extended the sanctuary into the crossing or even into the nave. This required removing some of the front pews. As a result, the altar was more forward, but the newly extended sanctuary pushed the people away yet again. And, though there may no longer be an altar rail, the steps still form a barrier so that only the ministers ascend into the sanctuary.

Many recently constructed churches begin with the plan of an altar standing forward in a sanctuary built as a centre-thrust stage. Typically the altar occupies the central place on such a stage. A more recent version arranges the altar, lectern and chair along a 'liturgical peninsula', a raised platform with seating on three sides.

Unfortunately, few parish communities drew inspiration from the Roman basilicas that have free-standing altars not sur-rounded by sanctuaries or altar rails. Those altars are set back or forward from the geographical centre of each basilica where other actions occur such as ordinations. Imagine a parish altar on a platform high enough to be seen, yet so small that it is in the midst of the people who come into direct contact with this table as they share the Lord's Supper.

The basilicas lack one element that featured prominently in the liturgical renewal after Vatican II: an ambo for the proclamation of the Word of God. In the medieval era, these basilicas had free-standing ambos in the midst of the nave for the proclamation of the scriptures. During the fourteenth-century Renaissance, these ambos were dismantled as medieval accretions in accord with the new aesthetic of wide open spaces. The ritual proclamation of scripture in Latin from such ambos had long been less effective pastorally.

Given the ecumenical renewal and development of the Liturgy of the Word in the vernacular following Vatican II, now is the time to reclaim the ambo tradition. This tradition differs from the use of a lectern in significant ways. In most parishes, the scriptures are proclaimed from a lectern in the sanctuary, whereas an ambo is typically located in the midst of the people, in the nave. A lectern, no matter how monumental, does not have the symbolic structure of an ambo, which is designed with an image of the empty tomb from which the Good News of the Resurrection is proclaimed in response to the command of the angel to the myrrh-bearing women: 'He is not here; for he has been raised ... go quickly and tell his disciples' (Matthew 28.6–7, *NRSV*).

Two important surviving ambos are at *Santa Maria in Cosmedin* and *San Clemente*, Rome. During the early twentieth century, an ambo was built at Westminster Cathedral. There you can see that the undercroft is empty, as if to say, 'He is not here', and, above on the balustrade, a bas-relief of the victorious lamb that was slain gives the positive interpretation of the empty tomb beneath. All scripture proclaimed from such an empty tomb is interpreted in light of the Resurrection of Christ.

St John Lateran and St Paul Outside the Walls challenge parishes and religious communities to reassess the use of the centre-thrust stage and expansive, segregated sanctuaries. They suggest a more dispersed and so dynamic arrangement that includes a free-standing altar on its own platform as small as absolutely necessary. This may allow for seating all the way around the altar, as in the Roman basilicas. Setting the altar back or forward from the geographical centre frees this central space for other ritual activity such as anointings, Communion and marriage. The presider's chair may be situated on its own small platform and used once again as the place for teaching, of which the pulpit was but an extension.

The first proper ambo built in Britain in the last century is at the new Church of Stanbrook Abbey, Wass, North Yorkshire. This older tradition could be reclaimed by constructing a free-standing ambo in the midst of the people. Such would allow a procession with the Gospel book from altar to ambo, and the movement of the assembly from the Liturgy of the Word to the Eucharistic Liturgy. A centre-thrust stage promotes visual participation, a fuller ritual participation may strengthen Christians for daily life and promote Christian unity (*Constitution on the Sacred Liturgy*, 1).

To Do

- Consider constructing a free-standing ambo designed as an empty tomb in the midst of the people for the proclamation of the scriptures
- Keep the central space empty for people to enjoy and for anointings, weddings and funerals
- Reduce the altar platform so that people can come into direct contact with this table where they share the Lord's Supper

Archbasilica of Our Most Holy Saviour, St John Lateran, Rome

The altar and transverse nave of the Archbasilica of Our Most Holy Saviour, St John Lateran, Rome. The cathedral's main nave and apse are developed for the celebration of liturgy. The transept is a secondary nave with the tabernacle prominent against its far wall (right). Both naves are used as one space for major liturgies.

The photographer in the picture is centred in the crossing of both naves, while the altar and ciborium are set forward toward the head of the nave, rather than being set back toward the apse. Four pillars support a ciborium over the altar which is set forward so that the gifts are placed directly under the centre of the ciborium.

This arrangement offers a possible corrective to many church renovations in which the altar was brought forward to be closer to the people and placed centrally in a raised sanctuary that was extended so far into the nave that the front pews had to be removed, thereby pushing the people away yet again. The development of a largely empty sanctuary, almost a *piazza* around the altar, is challenged by this ancient and venerable model of an altar whose platform is narrowly limited yet situated forward.

IV

THE RITUAL MODEL

Font – ambo – altar

22

BECOMING CHRISTIANS

The design of a church or chapel can be an expression of the liturgy celebrated there. This was admirably illustrated on a visit to a convent chapel converted from a stable. The warm welcome from the sisters was mirrored in the layout of their place of worship.

Fr James Leachman rang the bell of the Georgian estate house and peered inside, then said: 'I see a sister, and she is smiling!' Sr Mary Thomas never stopped smiling as she recounted her story over tea, how she came from Trinidad, taught for nine years as a Dominican, and then, after pursuing her career, she confirmed once again her vocation, this time at *Mater Ecclesiae* Convent, at Monks Kirby, established for women whose vocations come later in life. Her warm and personal welcome set the tone for the workshop we had come to give on how to welcome Catholics back into the practice of their faith. We gave the presentations to lay leaders of the Rugby deanery of the Archdiocese of Birmingham so that they in turn might welcome Catholics back. Such is best taught, we found, by extending a warm and personal welcome to these parish leaders as a means of confirming their own natural inclination to do so toward others.

When I had a free moment, I slipped into the sisters' chapel, which their foundress Sr Rose had designed and their master craftsman, Eddie, converted from the estate stable. The chapel offered another lesson in welcome, one built into the structure of the chapel itself. The natural wood beams arching to hold up the ceiling were graceful in this otherwise humble chapel with walls of white stucco better suited to contemplative prayer than to prayerful activity. I looked around and saw what one might expect, the tabernacle was front and centre, the altar in front of that, the chair to one side and the lectern to the other. This vernacular arrangement was well done but otherwise as expected, until I looked down.

The Amtico-brand floor had an inlay pattern that showed the path from the offset door to the centre aisle, where the pathway ran the length of the church towards the altar. Not only did the simple inlay design establish the centre aisle as a processional way, it also established the areas outside the centre aisle on both sides as places of rest, where chairs are provided for people to pause and hear the Word of God before resuming their journey towards the altar.

As I approached, immediately before the altar I saw a large starburst of wood inlaid into the floor, where people stand to receive Communion, where the sisters make their profession, where the deceased rest in vigil. The much larger altar was not centred on top of this starburst, as in many churches where the altar occupies the central position. Rather, the starburst was fully in front of the altar and there formed an *axis mundi*, an axis of the world, that is, a vertical axis where our relationship with God is mediated sacramentally in vocational profession, Communion and repose.

I was delighted to hear that the flooring was pieced together from a manufacturer's kit and so could easily be replicated by any church community. It takes only the insight and willing-ness to express in design the ritual activity of the liturgy already celebrated there.

This flooring became a metaphor also of members who are returning to the practice of their faith. From the door there is just a slight jog to the centre, but along the way there are places to rest and be refreshed by the Word of God proclaimed in the assembly, before completing the journey to share once again in Communion at the Lord's Table.

This metaphor works because it expresses well the transition in becoming Christians. If it were not a convent chapel but a parish church, the font could well be located at the entrance of the church, because that is where people become Christian through the Sacraments of Baptism and Confirmation. The initiation of a Christian is consummated when the newly baptized and confirmed are led to the altar and there share in Communion as a member of the body of Christ.

Although Baptism and Confirmation are not repeated, the passage to Communion is. Every Sunday and at every Eucharist, the procession normally passes the baptismal font, where the baptized use its waters to remind themselves of their dignity as Christians, and then passes down the centre aisle, pausing for a while in a place of rest for the refreshment of the Liturgy of the Word, before the pilgrimage arrives at its destination in shared Communion, and so renewed people return to live anew their daily lives in the world.

This experience illustrates that churches can be arranged according to the process of Christian initiation in which the Sacrament of Baptism with Confirmation leads to the Eucharist, and thereafter the Liturgy of the Word and the Eucharist are repeated time and again. Even a stable can be converted into a church if people are attentive to their personal experiences of becoming Christians and put their hand to noble design, yet simple material.

Churches are often designed in vernacular arrangements to meet the immediate expectations of someone who enters. Such a church places primary emphasis on the altar, lectern and chair, rather than on the three places of ritual encounter: the font, the ambo and the altar.

In their respective parts of a church, each of these is a monument both monumental and memorial: the baptismal font is the monument of a Christian's illumination in the baptistery, the ambo is the monument of the empty tomb from which we proclaim the Good News in the midst of the assembly gathered in the hall, and the altar on its dais is the monument of sharing in the gift of God's self in Christ. Thus illumination by light in baptism, inspiration by the Word and consummation in the Communion we share in the body and blood of Christ, these three establish the arrangement of a church.

Just as Sr Mary Thomas greeted us at the door with a warm welcome and told us her story as we shared tea, so also we helped others to welcome Christians back to the practice of their own faith with the same personal welcome. Designing churches, too, is to be based on the experience of coming to faith and sustaining faith through the sacraments of becoming Christians.

To Do

- Think about how you can highlight the procession from font to ambo and altar in your church
- Reflect on and enhance the way your parish welcomes all people who come
- Consider holding a series of sessions to extend a personal welcome to returning members

*Mother of the Church Congregation chapel
near Rugby, Warwickshire*

The floor design in the Mother of the Church Congregation chapel near Rugby, Warwickshire. The foundress, Sr Rose, chose this starburst design because 'this is where it all began', when Christ was born in a stable, and this chapel was built on the foundations of a stable. The design functions as an *axis mundi*, or pole of the earth, that anchors the community to its origin where their own transformation occurs in the divine encounter. The sisters receive Communion here, make their professions here and lie in state here.

This chapel has geo-thermal heating. A heat pump is set into the nearby earth and under the floor. Operating a water pump is the only ongoing expense needed to heat the chapel and nearby apartments. A wooden floor did not permit the heat to radiate up, so Amtico-brand vinyl flooring in wood grain was installed. Many parishes could follow this economic example and enhance their liturgical celebration.

The processional way is marked by the thin inset lines extending up from the bottom of the photo. These lines angle out to distinguish the place for the Liturgy of the Word in the nave from the area around the altar for the Eucharist.

AFTERWORD AND ONWARD

Finally the structure of this collection reveals the interrelationship among the chapters originally published individually in the Parish Practice page in *The Tablet* of London, many of them with an aim to be included in this collection.

In the final chapter we presented the ritual model, which is an attempt to establish a set of principles that may guide the design and construction of churches. It is called the ritual model because it considers the arrangement of a church beginning not with the more typical trio of altar, lectern, chair. The ritual model begins rather with the process of becoming a Christian, first in the water bath and anointing leading to shared Communion around the Lord's table, and thereafter in the process of maturing as a Christian by the celebration of the Liturgy of the Word and the Eucharistic Liturgy. Thus we first presented five chapters on Baptism, then five on the Liturgy of the Word, and one specifically on the Eucharist, which is nevertheless mentioned in several other chapters.

The ritual model uses the movement of sunlight within a church as a basis for considering the arrangement of processions and places of rest along three axes established by the light. Sunrise and sunset establish the major axis from the door to the altar. Along this axis the faithful go to meet Christ, the one coming. The place of their encounter is marked on the floor by an *axis mundi* or 'pole of the world' that extends to the height of the midday sun from its opposite, the nadir below. This is the axis of personal transformation as Christians come to share in divine life. The midday sun shining across the church establishes the third axis, the minor axis spanning the breadth of the church. This axis is used for proclaiming the Gospel from the ambo located on the side of the church of the midday sun so that the lector may stand facing with the sun's rays shining across the church to proclaim the Good News across the church.

The fundamental goal of the ritual model is to promote the full, conscious and active participation of the faithful in liturgy, which is first achieved when people understand the two-part structure of the liturgy. The two-part structure of the liturgy is expressed more clearly when the Liturgy of the Word is celebrated at the ambo and chairs, as distinct from the Eucharistic Liturgy celebrated at the altar.

The renewal of liturgy following the Second Vatican Council has inspired different arrangements of liturgical spaces. Some were based on an inadequately comprehensive design, and so achieved partial benefits.

The pastoral impetus, for example, to place the altar in the geographical centre of the space or of the assembly, unfortunately reduces the expression of the two-part structure of liturgy sometimes to nearly this sole focal point, thereby diminishing both the place for proclaiming the scripture and the *axis mundi* or 'pole of the world' as well as the processions. The free-standing altars of several Roman basilicas provide an example of an off-centre yet focal place for the Eucharistic Liturgy.

Another arrangement is based on two tables, one for the Eucharist and the other for the scripture. The two-part structure of the liturgy is evident in the construction of a table of the Word thereby bringing the proclamation of scripture to greater prominence. The two-table arrangement, however, interprets the proclamation of the scripture from a metaphorical table of the Word compared to the real eucharistic table, rather than according to its own proper symbolic structure.

The recovery of the ambo is key to a more comprehensive architectural design for liturgy. Ambos were used in the early Church, and over time their ritual use developed. An ambo provides a distinct place for the proclamation of scripture according to its own symbolic structure as the monument of the empty tomb. Medieval churches that preserve their ambo provide an example from their time that might benefit the celebration of the renewed liturgy, albeit adapted to current circumstances.

The divine encounter experienced in celebrating liturgy lies at the core of this book. The ritual model understands the art and architecture as an icon of the Church at prayer. The artistic narrative and architectural design both support the ritual action and interpret its meaning.

May this debut of the ritual model inspire parish communities to reflect on their celebration of liturgy and its meaning in their lives so that they may come to a fuller ritual expression and so share more fully in divine life by becoming more fully human.

BIBLIOGRAPHY

Original publication of articles found in this book

LEACHMAN, J. G., 'A time to be born', *The Tablet* (15 March 2008) 19 (here, article 3).

_____, 'Assembled as one', *The Tablet* (5 September 2009) 17 (here, article 7).

_____, 'Church of the senses', *The Tablet* (20 April 2013) 12 (here, article 5).

_____, 'Make a gift of your ministry', *The Tablet* (2 January 2010) 18 (here, article 8).

_____, 'Raise up the word', *The Tablet* (20 February 2010) 19 (here, article 10).

_____, 'Towards the enduring city', *The Tablet* (12 January 2013) 17 (here, article 2).

_____, 'Water for "new plants"', *The Tablet* (5 April 2008) 17 (here, article 4).

McCARTHY, D. P., 'A place for everyone', *The Tablet* (27 July 2013) 14 (here, article 21).

_____, 'Be guided by the light', *The Tablet* (27 April 2013) 13 (here, article 15).

_____, 'Becoming light', *The Tablet* (7 April 2012) 22 (here, article 1).

_____, 'Caught between heaven and earth', *The Tablet* (14 January 2012) 15 (here, article 13).

_____, 'Discoveries at an empty tomb', *The Tablet* (3 March 2012) 16 (here, article 9).

_____, 'From there to eternity', *The Tablet* (10 November 2012), 16 (here, article 14).

_____, 'Gather them in', *The Tablet* (25 May 2013) 13 (here, article 18).

————, 'Home from home', *The Tablet* (28 July 2012) 15 (here, article 22, 'Becoming Christians').

————, 'Intimate encounters', *The Tablet* (17/24 December 2011) 29 (here, article 12).

————, 'It's the taking part', *The Tablet* (6 October 2012) 16 (here, article 16).

————, 'Mix and Match', *The Tablet* (5 May 2012) 16 (here, article 6).

————, 'Stand up for the Lord', *The Tablet* (25 August 2012) 13 (here, article 20).

————, 'Table of good contents', *The Tablet* (29 June 2013) 16 (here, article 19).

————, 'Threshold of transcendence', *The Tablet* (7 September 2013) 16 (here, article 17).

————, 'To and from the living waters', *The Tablet* (16 June 2012) 12 (here, article 11).

Works cited

AUGUSTINUS AURELIUS, *Confessionum Libri XIII*, ed. L. Verheijen (Corpus christianorum series latina 27), Brepols, Turnhout 1981.

BENEDICT XVI, *Jesus of Nazareth: The Infancy Narratives*, tr. P. J. Whitmore, Random House (Image Books), New York 2012.

ELIOT, T. S., *Four Quartets: Burnt Norton*.

EPHRAEM SYRUS, *Ephrem the Syrian, Hymns*, ed. tr. K. E. McVey (Classics of Western Spirituality), Paulist Press, New York 1989.

General Instruction of the Roman Missal, ed. Catholic Bishops' Conference of England and Wales, Catholic Truth Society, London 2010 (*GIRM*).

The Holy Bible Containing the Old and New Testaments with the Apocryphal/Deuterocanonical Books, New Revised Standard Version, Oxford University Press, New York–Oxford 1989 (*NRSV*).

JOHN PAUL II, 'Post-synodal Apostolic Exhortation on the vocation and the mission of the lay faithful in the church and in the world', *Christifideles laici* (30 December 1988).

McCARTHY, D. P., 'Rediscovering Evening Prayer', *The Tablet* (5 June 2004) 16.

Missale Romanum ex decreto Sacrosanti Oecumenici Concilii Vaticani II instauratum auctoritate Pauli PP. VI promulgatum Ioannis Pauli PP. II cura recognitum, Editio typica tertia emendata, Typis Vaticanis, Città del Vaticano ³ᵉᵐ2008.

New American Bible, revised edition, Confraternity of Christian Doctrine, Inc., Washington DC 2001 (*RNAB*), accessed on 9 December 2015 from: http://www.usccb.org/bible/books-of-the-bible/ also available at: http://www.vatican.va/archive/ENG0839/_INDEX.HTM

The Roman Missal renewed by decree of the Most Holy Second Ecumenical Council of the Vatican, promulgated by authority of Pope Paul VI, and revised at the direction of Pope John Paul II, Catholic Truth Society, London 2010 (*RM 2011*).

SCHAMA, S., *The Power of Art*, The Bodley Head 2009, 400.

VATICAN II, in *Decrees of the Ecumenical Councils*, 2 vols, ed. N. Tanner, Sheed & Ward – Georgetown University Press, London-Washington 1990 (*DEC*).

Related Articles

McCARTHY, D. P., 'Fit for a nuptial feast', *The Tablet* (5 November 2011) 16.

_____, 'Happiness without end', *The Tablet* (29 March 2008) 16.

_____, 'Return to the font', *The Tablet* (30 April 2011) 14.

_____, 'Sacred exchanges', *The Tablet* (22/29 December 2007) 28–29.

_____, 'Unity through the Spirit', *The Tablet* (2 August 2008) 18.

VALENZIANO, C., 'Liturgical Architecture', in *Liturgical Time and Space*, ed. A. J. Chupungco (Handbook for Liturgical Studies 5), Liturgical Press (A Pueblo Book), Collegeville MN, pp. 381–396.

INDEX OF IMAGES BY
CHURCH

all indices compiled by
Br. Sixtus Roslevich OSB
St Louis Abbey, Missouri

INDEX OF SCRIPTURE

All citations are from the New Revised Standard Version unless noted.

INDEX OF CHRISTIAN
LITERATURE

INDEX OF PLACE NAMES

INDEX OF PEOPLE

INDEX OF SUBJECTS